BUILDING A CITY CHURCH

The Kensington Temple Vision

BUILDING A CITY CHURCH

The Kensington Temple Vision

by Colin W Dye

Building a City Church

Published by Dovewell Publications/Kingsway Publications.

ISBN 1-89844-400-5

Back cover photograph by Sylvan Mason
Front cover illustration by Cornelius Browne

Dovewell Publications
Kensington Park Road
London W11 3BY

Kingsway Publications Ltd
Lottbridge Drove
Eastbourne
E. Sussex BN23 6NR

Printed in Great Britain for
Dovewell/Kingsway Publications Ltd
by PrintKings Ltd
14 Steele Road
London NW10 7AS

Dedicated
to my wife
Amanda
and my daughters
Elizabeth and Laura
without whom my life would be poorer
and for whom I will always be grateful.

ACKNOWLEDGEMENTS

I am privileged to have the support of a talented group of people at Kensington Temple, many of whom have made a valuable contribution to the writing of this book. In fact, the whole congregation could be said to have played a part because of their encouragement and the way they have owned the vision. However, there are a few who have been closer to me than many others both in advice and physical preparation up to the time this book was sent to the printer. They are, in alphabetical order, William Atkinson, Christopher Cartwright, Stephen Jones, my secretary Julia Osborne and Alistair Taylor, who have helped to edit, and Brenda Wesley, who has not only helped edit the book, but has typeset and prepared the final copy for the printer. My colleague and friend, Jack Hywel-Davies, has not only provided the foreword but is a constant source of inspiration and encouragement.

CONTENTS — Page

Acknowledgments 7
Foreword by Jack Hywel-Davies 11
Introduction 15

PART 1 GOD'S HEART FOR THE CITY

1 The City of God 21
2 God's Plan for Cities 25
3 Christian Witness in the City 31
4 Faith for the City 37

PART 2 THE CITY CHURCH

5 What is a City Church? 43
6 The City Church Today 51
- Apostolic
- Large
- Visible
- Powerful
- Resourceful
- Organised
- Multicultural
- Effective

7 The Kensington Temple City Church 75

PART 3 MOBILISATION

8 Getting Involved 93

- Workmen
- Ploughmen
- Watchmen awake!
- The watchmen ministry
- Fishermen
- Calling all church planters!
- Power cell discipleship

9 Money Matters 139

10 Christian Unity 153

11 Time for Action! 161

FOREWORD by Jack Hywel-Davies

This is a powerful book.

It is powerful because it contains God-given insights to the author for the establishment and development of city churches as the twentieth century merges into the twenty-first. It is powerful because it also carries the weight of the writer's experience. It is powerful because it relates one of the Spirit's most exciting developments for such a time as this.

If anyone is tempted to falter at the threshold of this vision, let me reassure him from my personal and privileged viewpoint that this vision is already on its way to fulfilment under the ministry of Colin Dye.

I have served in different capacities in the Church for more than half a century. Yet I do not recall being more inspired by any other book in all that time. Indeed, I would dare to say that I am excited by the prospects of church expansion it describes.

Over the past few years I have been looking into the history of revivals, especially those of the eighteenth, nineteenth and twentieth centuries. I have noticed that one thing common to every one of them has been an unusual amount of spiritual hunger. Smith Wigglesworth used to say that he was like a spoilt child when it came to spiritual food; he was always hungry for more. This has been a major emphasis I have observed in Colin Dye's ministry. His prayer life is paramount and is placed above even his gifted preaching and prophetic ministry.

This book is written against the background of a nation suffering moral and spiritual decay, where even church leaders are failing to give the nation the medicine necessary for its recovery. Colin challenges us towards a strategy given to him by God, based on the expansion of the early Church.

Of course, there have been great revivals in the past. God has raised up many of his servants to lead nations back to him. But one of the sad results of these revivals has been the subsequent falling away, and this has exercised the thoughts of many writers. In the case of the 1904 Welsh Revival, which seems to have been short lived, there was a marked absence of preaching, in contrast to the days that followed the outpouring of the Holy Spirit on the day of Pentecost described in Acts 2. What happened then? Luke tells us that after Peter's sermon, "those who accepted his message were baptised..." and "devoted themselves to the apostles' teaching and to the fellowship, to the breaking of bread and to prayer" (vv. 41,42).

The questions then arise, "Who was responsible for this? Could it have happened spontaneously?" or, "Was there an immediate structure to ensure that the young converts were fed?" I am convinced it was the latter, and here in this book the author describes how this can be the experience of the Church today. And that means in the city where you live.

This book is not an argument for "big is beautiful" versus "small is beautiful." Rather, it shows how both are beautiful when experienced together.

I can well imagine some will be uneasy with the author's comment that, "Our cities will never be won by small, inward-looking parochial churches with a 'village' mentality. We must see the raising up of vast city churches reaching across entire metropolitan conurbations" (page 43).

The sceptic may well cite existing or past city churches where the individual is lost and alone. One of my former tutors at theological college, after a visit to such churches in America, began preaching that churches should be limited to twenty members. But the exciting prospect of this vision at Kensington Temple is that individual groups making up the 6,000 can comprise cells of even fewer than twenty.

The apostle Paul always made for large cities, centres of communication, highlighted by his attention to Rome (all roads lead to Rome). These centres are also seats of power, and if the Church is to exercise its moral as well as its spiritual leadership, they are the ideal places to be. As Canon Michael Green writes in his book *Evangelism in the Early Church:* "Paul's strategy was urban. He made for the centres... The Acts of the Apostles records his visit to city after city of importance: Antioch, the third city in the Empire; Philippi, the Roman *colonia*; Thessalonica, the principal metropolis of Macedonia; Corinth, the capital of Greece under Roman administration; Paphos, the centre of Roman rule in Cyprus; Ephesus, the principal city of of the province of Asia. It is hard to escape the conclusion that this succession of cities... was not hit on by accident. It was part of a definite plan for planting the good news in key positions throughout the Empire. The climax of his urban policy [was] Rome."

In this book, Colin Dye says that if we are to see this vision realised, "we are going to have to drop some of our old ideas of church life. We must make room for new concepts which are consistent with what God is doing today." (page 43)

If I may be allowed to enter a personal line here, I have been involved in publishing as editor and publisher for the best part of forty years, and when I found my salesmen (handling books every day of their lives) becoming excited about a book I invariably sat up and took notice. My friend, John Paculabo, chief executive of Kingsway Publications, told me that when he showed the early rough draft of this book to his marketing men they responded with enthusiasm. They believed this book was especially for the Church today and were eager to become part of its distribution.

What greater recommendation can be given to any book? I pray that God will make it a blessing and a source of inspiration to your community.

INTRODUCTION

I have had the privilege of being at Kensington Temple for over twenty years. When I first came to the church, shortly after my conversion in 1971, the congregation was around 300 strong. Over the years, as a church member, a deacon, an elder and as a pastor, I have witnessed it grow first under the leadership of Eldin Corsie and then subsequently, Wynne Lewis, to a church of over 6,000. Now, in the 1990's, as Senior Pastor, I am totally convinced, despite that phenomenal growth, that we have not yet begun to see what God has in store for London. I want us to set our sights higher, boldly taking possession of the hope of tomorrow and moving into our destiny in God.

I want every member of our church to be aligned to the will of God for London and to be equipped to work together for his purposes in this great city. There is no limit to what we can do for God together as we cry out to the Father for his grace to be poured out upon our city and as we fight side by side in the Holy Spirit's great offensive against the works of Satan.

This book is an attempt to write down the vision that the Lord has given me for Kensington Temple. The object, in the first instance, was to inform, inspire and motivate all in Kensington Temple with this vision so that together we can play our part in this exciting move of God. I was challenged to do this by the words the Lord spoke to Habakkuk the prophet.

> *Then the LORD replied: "Write down the revelation and make it plain on tablets so that a herald may run with it."*
>
> *(Habakkuk 2:2)*

However, since beginning the project, almost a year ago, I have met hundreds of pastors and church leaders from London and all over Britain who also sense what I have been sensing. God is

PART ONE -

GOD'S HEART FOR THE CITY

1

THE CITY OF GOD

Then I saw a new heaven and a new earth, for the first heaven and the first earth had passed away, and there was no longer any sea. [2]I saw the Holy City, the new Jerusalem, coming down out of heaven from God, prepared as a bride beautifully dressed for her husband. [3]And I heard a loud voice from the throne saying, "Now the dwelling of God is with men, and he will live with them. They will be his people, and God himself will be with them and be their God. [4]He will wipe every tear from their eyes. There will be no more death or mourning or crying or pain, for the old order of things has passed away."

(Revelation 21:1-4)

Every Christian longs for the Holy City, the New Jerusalem, the heavenly kingdom come down to earth. That city is going to carry the full manifestation of God's presence and glory. God will dwell among his people forever. From his throne at the heart of that city, God will govern in absolute righteousness, justice and purity. There will be no pain, hatred or violence, no more death, mourning or crying: only fulness of joy.

He wants us to bring something of the language and customs, the culture and climate of the city of God into our life on earth. All this is by way of foretaste, not of fulness, but we can make a difference to society. We can see something of the city of God on earth now and we are called to fulfil our duty as citizens of that city while we are here on earth.

2

GOD'S PLAN FOR CITIES

For many years we western Christians have been guilty of turning our backs on the cities of the world. We have seen them only as centres of sin, exploitation and moral decay. We prefer the cleaner atmosphere of the suburbs, coming into the inner cities only for business or entertainment. We have Christianised the complacency of the middle classes and sacrificed Christ's compassion for the poor and needy on the altar of compromise, preferring a more comfortable, less challenging life-style.

And yet nothing could be further from the heart of God. God cares for the cities with an intensity beyond description. He has an irrepressible love for people. Where the masses are to be found, there is God also, longing to reach out and to touch them, to bring his healing to their hurting lives and to break in with his love and forgiveness. The cities of today are prime candidates for an outpouring of the grace of God that is at the heart of our message. As the apostle Paul puts it,

> *But where sin increased, grace increased all the more...*
>
> *(Romans 5:20)*

The Bible shows that God has a definite plan for the cities of the world. Cities stand before him as unique entities, each with its own special character. This is strange to many of us who like to emphasise the individual nature of our faith, but while God does deal with us as individuals, he also deals with groups of people: families, tribes, nations and cities.

The greatest example in the Bible of God's concern for cities is his care for Jerusalem. God set his love upon this city and chose it for a very special role. Isaiah's call for intercession for the city of Jerusalem shows God's plan for her.

> *I have posted watchmen on your walls, O Jerusalem; they will never be silent day or night. You who call on the Lord, give yourselves no rest, and give him no rest till he establishes Jerusalem and makes her the praise of the earth.*
>
> *(Isaiah 62:6,7)*

He promised to cause Jerusalem to be praised in all the earth, using her to bless all nations. The prophecy was fulfilled, in part, when in the days of the apostles the message of the gospel was taken from Jerusalem to the far corners of the Roman empire.

However, God's plans for cities do not end with Jerusalem or with the Jewish people. God's purpose in choosing Abraham was that everyone should be blessed through his Seed, who is Jesus Christ. In choosing one man, God set his love upon all men. God's choice of Israel was not to exclude the other nations of the earth, but to establish Israel as a light to all nations so that they too would come to know him. Similarly, when God chose Jerusalem, he demonstrated his heart's desire for all cities, showing that he wants to reveal his praise and glory through all the cities of the earth. That is the great call of the Holy Spirit for this hour. By the end of the decade, three quarters of the world's population will live in cities. We cannot abandon them but must believe God for them.

God's call to Nineveh is an outstanding example o compassion for the cities of the world. A pagan idolatry, Nineveh was perhaps the most wicked c ancient world. Yet God had compassion and sent J preach to Nineveh and warn of the coming judgmen But Jonah was so horrified at the thought of God's word being brought to a pagan nation and an enemy of Israel that he refused to go. Instead, he fled from the Lord and ran in the opposite direction to the call of God on his life. When he finally obeyed the Lord and delivered God's word to the city, Nineveh repented. Angry with God, Jonah began to argue,

> *"O LORD, is this not what I said when I was still at home? That is why I was so quick to flee to Tarshish. I knew that you are a gracious and compassionate God, slow to anger and abounding in love, a God who relents from sending calamity. Now, O LORD, take away my life, for it is better for me to die than to live."*
>
> *(Jonah 4:2,3)*

God replied,

> *"But Nineveh has more than a hundred and twenty thousand people who cannot tell their right hand from their left, and many cattle as well. Should I not be concerned about that great city?"*
>
> *(Jonah 4:11)*

Jonah was so angry with the Lord that he wanted to die. But God in his mercy was pleased to save Nineveh and subsequently dealt with Jonah, pointing out that Jonah had more compassion for a garden plant than for that city. Sometimes we can get just as preoccupied with our own little concerns and comforts, caring more about our gardens in the leafy suburbs than for the hungry hearts of the people in our crowded cities. Perhaps there are many 'Jonahs' out there, running away from the dirt and poverty of our inner cities and hiding from the ugliness of human beings so obviously rebelling against God and out of relationship with each other.

It is time we faced God's plan for the cities of our nations. There is a clear strategic element in God's dealing with cities. An invading army wanting to win a nation would not have any lasting success without conquering the cities. Once the cities are taken the nation falls. Britain's only hope is for its cities to be won for the Lord, and for God's grace and power to be made manifest in our great metropolitan areas. This is especially true for London.

Grace for London

Some time ago, I was troubled by what some prophetic voices were claiming about the nation. God, it seemed, had nothing good to say about Britain and all we could expect was severe judgment. I came before the Lord and asked for his word for London. In response, the Holy Spirit impressed an image on my mind's eye. I saw an angelic figure holding a massive bowl filled with liquid high over the city of London. The bowl was roughly the same size as the M25, the large orbital motorway encircling the entire metropolitan area of London. My first thought was of the bowls of God's wrath in the book of Revelation. I cried out, "That's it! We're done for now!"

But this was not what the Lord was showing me. As I looked more closely I saw that the angel was not too concerned with holding the bowl steady, since when he moved slightly the bowl began to rock to and fro causing the liquid to splash over the edges. When this liquid fell upon London, way down below, extraordinary things began to happen. I saw people stand up and shake off their chains, their faces lighting up with joy as they sang, shouted and danced with great exuberance and freedom. I said, "Lord what is going on here? What's happening?" and I felt the Lord say to me, "That's my grace. I have still yet more grace to pour out upon London."

That picture filled me with such joy. God's longing, even for the most wicked places, is to pour out his grace and mercy. The blood of Jesus Christ has been shed for every man, woman and child in our cities. Our job is to proclaim that fact loud and clear within the hearing of everyone, and to call them to repent and believe so that they might receive his forgiveness. There is still hope for our nation and that hope rests in our hands.

3

CHRISTIAN WITNESS IN THE CITY

> *"You are the salt of the earth. But if the salt loses its saltiness, how can it be made salty again? It is no longer good for anything, except to be thrown out and trampled by men.*
>
> *[14]You are the light of the world. A city on a hill cannot be hidden. [15]Neither do people light a lamp and put it under a bowl. Instead they put it on its stand, and it gives light to everyone in the house. [16]In the same way, let your light shine before men, that they may see your good deeds and praise your Father in heaven."*
>
> *(Matthew 5:13-16)*

Imagine what London would be like if it was full of Christians who knew how to live and share together but didn't cocoon themselves in cosy church meetings. What a difference it would make to London if Christians really got involved in the life of the city, going into places like Kings Cross, Earls Court and Soho to show God's love to the people. Similar things could be said of every major city in Britain. Think of the impact if we tangibly demonstrated God's love in the vast, impersonal housing estates in our cities, many of which have over 80% single parent families living in them and where most children have lost all contact with their father.

For a long time, Christians have been confused and often divided over the issue of social action. Some have stressed a 'social gospel' which practically reduces the entire message of good news to good works. Evangelism is soft peddled and social concerns crowd out the message of the cross and forgiveness. On the other hand, many evangelical and charismatic Christians have forgotten the social implications of the gospel. God cares about people as people and not as disembodied souls that need saving. He is concerned for the whole man, spirit, soul and body.

> *May God himself, the God of peace, sanctify you through and through. May your whole spirit, soul and body be kept blameless at the coming of our Lord Jesus Christ.*
>
> *(1 Thessalonians 5:23)*

Paul's words here are entirely consistent with Jesus' own call for us to be practical, demonstrating a life of good deeds in the community,

> *"...let your light shine before men, that they may see your good deeds and praise your Father in heaven."*
>
> *(Matthew 5:16)*

But if social action is so important, what is its relationship to evangelism, and how can we avoid confusing the two? How can we make sure one is not overemphasised to the detriment of the other? Jesus Christ made clear what the church was really called to do. His final words to the disciples prior to his ascension into heaven were unmistakable.

> *"Go into all the world and preach the good news to all creation."*
>
> *(Mark 16:15)*

Evangelism and world mission is our calling and must be our priority. Nothing must detract from it in any way.

However, Jesus calls us not only to preach good news, but also to be good news. If our faith is not accompanied by corresponding actions, then a credibility gap opens, and most non-Christians will never bridge it. What we say and what we do must add up. Therefore true Christian witness in the city will include both evangelism and social action.

When Jesus said that we were the salt of the earth and light of the world, he was referring to our identity as Christians. He did not say, "You should be salt and light". Rather, he said, "You *are* salt and light." This is fundamental to our relationship with Christ himself. If we belong to him, then of necessity we are different, not being of the same material, so to speak, as the world. Therefore, for our Christian faith to have any credibility, it must be demonstrated by a certain quality which cannot fail to affect society. Otherwise, as Jesus said, the salt has lost its saltiness and the light has been hidden.

Jesus' call for external actions consistent with a professed faith is identical to the word of prophets of the Old Testament who were raised up to speak to Israel and Judah. They were fearless in their denunciation of the sins of the nation and uncompromising in their call for behaviour consistent with faith in God. They would go to the palace and denounce the sins committed right at the throne of the nation. They were men who knew God and were given a special anointing from the Lord to reflect his heart and his passion for truth, righteousness and holiness as well as his compassion and love.

One such prophet was Micah. Called by the Lord many centuries ago, his message is of great relevance for us today as we focus on the cities of the world. He gives us one of the clearest summaries of what God requires of people who would walk with him.

> *He has showed you, O man, what is good. And what does the LORD require of you? To act justly and to love mercy and to walk humbly with your God.*
>
> *(Micah 6:8)*

This is the call of God for urban Christians everywhere. If we had a generation of people like Micah living in London, the salt would regain its saltiness and the light would really begin to shine. We would be that city set on a hill that cannot be hidden. I am setting forth a dream here, but if we all take up the challenge of Micah it can become a reality. I am sure this reflects something of God's heart for the city. He wants a covenant community that represents him to the world in obedience to his will.

James puts his finger on it in his open letter to Christians,

> *Religion that God our Father accepts as pure and faultless is this: to look after orphans and widows in their distress and to keep oneself from being polluted by the world.*
>
> *(James 1:27)*

James doesn't tell us to escape from our cities or to stay in our cosy churches. He calls us to take God's love to the people. James' words encourage us to get involved in the city and yet to remain pure from its pollutions. The great challenge is to live holy lives while being barraged every day with so much uncleanliness and temptation to compromise.

As Christians we need to put away everything that hinders the free course of God's Spirit in our lives. We must cleanse ourselves from the pollution and only then will we be qualified to lovingly lead people away from the futile things that are keeping them from seeing the grace of God poured into their lives.

Jesus calls us to live among people as lambs among wolves, to live such a quality of life that people see him in us. On a personal note, I want to encourage you, if you are struggling with issues in your life, for the Holy Spirit is within you. Don't believe the devil's lie. You are part of the solution because Jesus lives within you and greater is he that is within you than he that is within the world (1 John 4:4). God will give you strength to overcome temptation, and will set you free to be a vessel of the Holy Spirit. He promised that those who believed in him would have streams of living water flowing out from within (John 7:38). Let that power flow out every day like cool, refreshing streams touching the dry and barren lives of thirsty people. Your city needs to see a Spirit filled church reaching out with the purity and love of Christ, carrying his concern to every borough and every street.

Some time ago, God gave one of our church elders a prophetic revelation for us. He saw in his mind's eye a picture of thousands of people coming into the Kensington Temple building like people attending a football match. Across their foreheads was written, "Hearers of the Word". Then he saw the whole company of people turn around and march out. They had come as a rabble and now left as an army, this time with "Doers of the Word" written across their foreheads.

I have held onto this vision for years and I believe that the time is very close when God is going to fulfil it. No longer are we going to be just hearers of the word of God, but we are going to rise up in a new spirit of faith, marching out through the doors of our churches with our heads held high, as part of his army, doing his word.

We believe Jesus is alive and that he wants to show his love to the world through us. We accept he has called us to be salt and light in society. We know that he saves sinners and heals the sick. Let's now go out and show the world that these things are true. Let's really begin to shine for Jesus, right where we are in our sphere of influence. We must do it with wisdom, grace and dignity, but let's stop merely talking about it. It is time for action.

4

FAITH FOR THE CITY

If we are faithful, in the coming days we will see God move in our cities as never before. Let us, like Moses, stand on the mountain and catch a glimpse of what is possible. Picture with me what we could well be witnessing this decade.

Instead of Pavarotti in the park, we will have live television coverage of prayer and prophecy from Hyde Park! People will hold open prayer meetings in cafes, sharing the gospel freely. Men and women will weep with repentance and joy as they come to Christ by the hundreds on street corners. Churches will be full.

On Cup Final day we will see the footballers line up and, after the national anthem, they will bow their heads and pray, every one of them baptised in the Holy Spirit! Later in the evening, Wembley Stadium will host a Christian pop concert and the bands will lead the gathered crowd in praise and worship as they minister to the Lord in song. People will be saved, healed and filled with the Holy Spirit right there in the stadium, so holy will be the music.

In the Houses of Parliament we will have the lifting of holy hands in the chambers. Members of the Government and of the Opposition will be meeting in the corridors to pray and intercede for the nation. They will meet in committee rooms to pray for the power of the Holy Spirit, that they may come to a consensus concerning issues of national and international significance. Petty party politics will be crucified along with the flesh. The interests of the nation, the kingdom of God and godliness will come first.

Why shouldn't we believe God for these things? As we watch the television news every day we cry out, "Why Lord?" But let us listen to the news that is coming from heaven and cry, "Why not, Lord?" All it takes is the faith to believe God and put his words into practice. God is asking for a generation who will say, "Yes, Lord. No matter what the cost, we hear and we obey."

Let us not be like the Israelites who failed to inherit the promised land through unbelief. They were poised to enter Canaan from the Desert of Paran. God had promised them on oath that he would give them the land. He had demonstrated that he was able and willing to do it in the miracles that he had performed in the land of Egypt. The great miracle of deliverance across the Red Sea had confirmed that he was with his people, that he had come down to deliver them and be faithful to his promises. From Sinai, he brought them to Kadesh Barnea. There, God told Moses to send spies in to assess Canaan. Two of them, Caleb and Joshua, came running back ahead of the others. They called together a praise band and said, "We can do it! We can take this land for the Lord. It is exactly as God said. It is a good land, flowing with milk and honey. God surely is with us, we can do it!" The other ten shouted them down and said, "Youthful exuberance and fanaticism. Let's tell you what it's really like: it's impossible. The cities are fortified; the armies are well trained; the inhabitants are giants, and we are grasshoppers."

Unbelief began to spread like a cancer through the camp. Moments before they were responding to the praise calls of Joshua and Caleb. They were beginning to enter into their destiny: to be taken from Egypt and brought into the land of Canaan. But now they were filled with unbelief, and so nobody entered the promised land until every one of that unbelieving generation had perished in the wilderness. Still God provided the pillars of fire by night and cloud by day; still the manna came and their clothes did not wear out. God kept them, loved them and provided for them, but he marginalised them.

There is a Canaan spread before us today in the 1990's. God is ready to give the cities into our hands in this generation. But he is waiting for a believing people who will look at the possibilities and say, "We will rise to take the city for Jesus!" It requires a believing people who will not shrink back but through faith and patience inherit the promises of God for the city.

PART TWO

THE CITY CHURCH

5

WHAT IS A CITY CHURCH?

We are on the threshold of a great outpouring of the Holy Spirit. God is ready to move in apostolic power within our cities and across the nations of the earth. But how prepared are we for the coming move of God? If God wants us to win our cities for him, how is it going to be done? What kind of church will be able to achieve it? Clearly God wants a strong, vibrant and powerful church acting as the body of Christ in the city, but what will that church look like?

It is my firm conviction that God will raise up a new phenomenon in the British church, and to see it happen we are going to have to drop some of our old ideas of church life. We must make room for new concepts which are consistent with what God is doing today. Our cities will never be won by small, inward-looking parochial churches with a 'village' mentality. We must see the raising up of vast city churches reaching across entire metropolitan conurbations.

These churches will have the spiritual authority necessary to challenge the spiritual powers holding captive the populations of our cities. City churches must come forth in the 1990's with such force that they sweep aside all opposition and change the spiritual climate of our nation. We must see governing churches built with enough authority to transform society's institutions, claiming entire cities and nations back for God.

What then is a city church? Quite simply, a city church comprises Christians functioning as the body of Christ in a city. When we read of churches in the New Testament, we tend to impose our modern concept of a local church onto the text. When we study the book of Acts and New Testament church history, we discover it could never have been that way. New Testament examples include the churches in Corinth, Ephesus and Jerusalem.

Corinth

> *To the church of God in Corinth, to those sanctified in Christ Jesus and called to be holy, together with all those everywhere who call on the name of our Lord Jesus Christ - their Lord and ours...*
>
> *(1 Corinthians 1:2)*

The church of a city was known by the name of the city it was located in, and was composed of the body of believers functioning citywide. The church of Corinth numbered many thousands and must have had many congregations gathering all over the city. They would have come together from time to time as one body in large gatherings, but they mainly met in smaller congregations which functioned fully as churches in their own right, while remaining a recognisable part of the whole body of Christ in Corinth. Church buildings, for public Christian worship, were not common before the third or fourth century, and up until that time churches would meet almost always in homes. This was certainly the pattern in Corinth as we see from 1 Corinthians.

Ephesus

> *The churches in the province of Asia send you greetings. Aquila and Priscilla greet you warmly in the Lord, and so does the church that meets at their house.*
>
> *(1 Corinthians 16:19)*

The situation was similar in Ephesus where there was also a large urban church with many thousands of people. When these New Testament churches were born, extraordinary miracles were commonplace. They steamrollered through and pulled down mighty principalities and satanic strongholds. Through the city church at Ephesus, the whole of Asia Minor was evangelised and the seven churches of Revelation came into being. Describing Paul's teaching ministry in the lecture hall of Tyrannus at Ephesus, Luke says,

> *This went on for two years, so that all the Jews and Greeks who lived in the province of Asia heard the word of the Lord.*
>
> *(Acts 19:10)*

Behind this outstanding missionary success there must have stood many congregations networking across the city and multiplying out from Ephesus. No tiny, narrow or inward-looking 'local' church could have done it. It was a dynamic, diverse and multi-faceted city church. There was a great citywide explosion of life that had a huge impact on the entire region as the shock waves shook the province of Asia.

Jerusalem

The Jerusalem church is another example of a great New Testament city church. As the religious capital of the world for the Jews, Jerusalem stood as a fortress needing to be taken, and was won for Christ by a city church. Revival hit the city and confounded its officials, sweeping scores of thousands into the kingdom of God. The structure of the Jerusalem church helps us to understand how city churches can function at different levels. There were at least three different levels of fellowship present in the Jerusalem church.

First, there were large celebrations. Thousands would come to worship daily at the Jewish time of prayer and gather afterwards, praising God in the temple courts. The apostles would then teach, much in the way Jesus had taught at Solomon's Colonnade. Thousands of people would meet in that way.

Secondly, they would probably also have met in larger households as congregations.

Finally, they would also have met as small groups in homes, breaking bread in table fellowship day by day.

> *Every day they continued to meet together in the temple courts. They broke bread in their homes and ate together with glad and sincere hearts, [47]praising God and enjoying the favour of all the people. And the Lord added to their number daily those who were being saved.*
>
> (*Acts 2:46,47*)

These three levels of fellowship have been identified by modern church growth analysts as cell, congregation and celebration meetings. Each has a valid part in the overall healthy functioning of church life. And, what is more, city churches are capable of sustaining each level, making use of the different dynamic released in them. The cell meetings are helpful for intimate fellowship and personal development. The congregational meetings offer the opportunity for wider fellowship and stronger witness to the community. The celebrations bring the whole body together for mass witness and the release of power through corporate prayer, praise and proclamation of the word of the Lord. These are the occasions when the entire church can stand together, hear the voice of the Lord together and move forward together as one body.

We have had a glimpse of the city churches of the New Testament, but a great deal has happened to the church since then. What about today? The circumstances of the modern church are barely recognisable in terms of early church life. There are thousands of denominations and modes of expression today. I am not saying that within a decade we are going to reverse this and there would be only one church in London called Kensington Temple!

Many object to any thought of going back to the New Testament pattern. I agree that we should be speaking more of New Testament principles than rigid patterns, but it is very clear to me that the Lord is restoring to the Church today much that has been lost down through the years. The endtime Church will be at least a New Testament church. I say, "at least," because I expect it to be much more. In short, if the New Testament shows the Church in its infancy, just imagine the Church in its maturity. Paul speaks of the Church which will be manifest in the end-time when he says that the ministries of the church are given,

> *...to prepare God's people for works of service, so that the body of Christ may be built up* [13]*until we all reach unity in the faith and in the knowledge of the Son of God and become mature, attaining to the whole measure of the fulness of Christ.* [14]*Then we will no longer be infants, tossed back and forth by the waves, and blown here and there by every wind of teaching and by the cunning and craftiness of men in their deceitful scheming.* [15]*Instead, speaking the truth in love, we will in all things grow up into him who is the Head, that is, Christ.*
>
> *(Ephesians 4:12-15)*

Clearly the apostle Paul was expecting the church to grow up. Obviously this refers to the state of the church at the coming of the Lord. Some argue that this "perfection" is not attainable. While I agree that perfection is not attainable, maturity is. God is surely going to grant his church that maturity before Jesus Christ returns. If the New Testament 'infant church' could achieve what we read of in the book of Acts, what will be the capabilities of the mature end-time church?

Already we are seeing even greater things taking place in some areas than those recorded in the Acts of the Apostles. I have seen greater numbers of people saved in a single meeting than were saved on the day of Pentecost. On that day it is recorded that 3,000 received Christ. This probably meant 5,000 to 8,000 people including the women and children, as it was usual for men only to be counted in New Testament times. I have been in meetings where more than 8,000 people have received Jesus Christ. Most of us, when we get to heaven, would probably like to ask Peter what it was like to preach and see more than 3,000 saved on the day of Pentecost. Peter would probably say, "I'll gladly answer you, but first tell me what was it like to live at the end of the twentieth century during the outpouring of the Holy Spirit and see hundreds of thousands saved in a single meeting." Just because it's not happening in Britain yet doesn't mean to say it's not going to happen. It is already happening, to some extent, in Nigeria, Brazil, South Korea, China and many other parts of the world, and it's going to happen in Britain as well. I believe it is going to happen in our cities.

We must raise our levels of expectation for new dimensions of church life today. If we are faithful, we will see new levels of faith and power, new patterns of church life and ministry and new authority that comes from the maturity God is bringing to the Church. This means that we will at least be a New Testament church with all the New Testament principles and dynamics fully operating, including the dynamic of a city church.

From these New Testament examples we can identify three main elements of a city church.

The city church is organised into smaller fully functioning self-contained and integral units: churches gathering all over the city.

The churches are recognisable as part of the larger whole: members of the body, with distinctive functions, but joined together as parts of the whole body.

The result is that all the Christians of the city move and act together as the body of Christ in the city.

Pitfalls

However, as soon as we try to apply New Testament teaching on the church, certain problems emerge. Excessive dogmatism is inappropriate in the matter of church government. The New Testament is more flexible than we think. There are great dangers in seeking to return to some "golden age" of church life that probably never existed in the first place, and even if it did, would not be applicable to what God is doing today. This is also true of our desire for a city church today. At every point in history where there has been a rigid organisational approach to building a city church it has been an unmitigated disaster. We are not seeking to build a monstrous megastructure, nor are we trying to impose rigid patterns upon ourselves or others. No doctrinaire approach could ever work as it would lead either to a form of spiritual imperialism (that is, taking captive and monopolising other churches) or it could lead to a gross form of spiritual elitism (that is, ignoring or rejecting other streams as invalid or less important than its your own). One cannot tear down all denominational barriers and boundaries in an attempt to impose a monolithic church over the city. The results would be disastrous.

A citywide church

A more accurate description of Kensington Temple is that we are seeking to become a citywide church, as one major stream flowing in the capital among other important streams. And we are looking for ways of flowing with other streams as part of the corporate river of God in London.

> *There is a river whose streams make glad the city of God, the holy place where the Most High dwells.*
>
> *(Psalm 46:4)*

Already, it is beginning to happen. We have joint celebrations held in large venues in London, in which different expressions of the body of Christ come together. There are citywide meetings for prayer, the Marches for Jesus, and many other joint initiatives for evangelism and witness. These are attempts to bring together the wider body of Christ in the city and to see something of Psalm 46:4 take place in London.

6

THE CITY CHURCH TODAY

How will these general principles of the city church help us in preparing a citywide strategy for today?

Making disciples

Obviously, winning a city to Christ begins with evangelism, but the job does not end when you have won a soul; it has only just begun. We are called to make disciples and to mature them into the image of Christ.

I am still challenged by the words of Canon James Wong visiting from Singapore. He said to us in 1987, "As this century began with revival in Wales reaching out to many parts of the earth, so the century will close with a revival beginning in London that shall touch the nations." He then went on prophesy that in order to play our part in its fulfilment, we had to be an effective disciple-making church.

This means that we must fully integrate new believers into the life of the body of Christ. We must follow the New Testament pattern of evangelism which resulted in adding fully functioning members to the church. Jesus Christ said, "I will build my church" (Matthew 16:18), and if we take his words seriously, it will mean working for both the growth of existing congregations and the planting of new ones. Many see the need for the former but find it hard to see the relevance of the latter.

Why plant churches?

I am somctimes told by pastors, "The last thing we need is more churches." Actually, nothing could be further from the truth. How can we speak of having enough churches when 90% of the population does not attend one? This is extreme 'maintenance mentality' and it has no place in the kingdom of God. We need 7,000 new churches in London if we are going to see the churchgoing population double within the next ten years. These were the findings of the Challenge 2000 congress held in Birmingham early in 1992. The congress, a British initiative coming from the DAWN 2000 strategy for discipling a whole nation, was attended by over 30 different denominations, many represented at national leadership level.

New churches are desperately needed to contain the new life that will come during the decade of evangelism. The existing churches simply will not be able to cope if this initiative is as fruitful as we believe. It is not just a matter of the size of existing church buildings. Many churches are simply not geared up to receive converts from the unchurched community.

The cultural gap that exists between those attending church and those who are totally unchurched is so vast that very few unchurched converts will be able to cross it. And if the churches were to change radically, they would immediately isolate their own people. We could point to some changes, but the reality is that they are not happening quickly enough. Some are asking the question, "Why should existing churches change if they are successfully meeting the needs of their existing members?" And even if we achieved the maximum adaptability possible, I doubt if there would be a sufficient variety of churches capable of reaching the diversity of cultures crying out for valid Christian expression in our cities.

The answer is for us to plant new churches as well as to grow our existing ones. New expressions of the body of Christ will be more adaptable in meeting the needs of new converts, many of them arising out of specific ministry to specific groups in the city. New churches will release the enormous untapped people resources sitting idle in our churches. This waste of spiritual gifts is scandalous.

Given all these advantages, we may be tempted to use church planting simply as a method of processing new converts. But it is an observable fact that a church planting programme is, in itself, one of the best methods of generating new converts. Dr Peter Wagner, the world renowned Christian author and church growth analyst, goes so far as to say, "The single most effective evangelistic methodology under heaven is planting new churches" (C Peter Wagner, *Church Planting for a Greater Harvest,* Regal Books, 1990, p.11). He bases his statement both on the Bible and what he has observed on the international church growth scene.

Much has yet to be worked out and prayerfully developed on the whole question of church planting, but there is already a large body of information available which can help shape our response to it and our involvement in it. Those with an active church planting policy are too often viewed with suspicion. But the work of God in the city is simply too important for us to hinder any valid advance of God's kingdom, no matter how it happens or where it comes from.

Church planting is not enough

Having said so much about church planting, I must make it clear that the Kensington Temple vision is not simply to plant churches all over London. We do have a target to see 2,000 churches planted by the year 2000, but the vision is to take our city for Jesus, and we will never do that simply by planting individual churches. We could plant 2,000 churches all over the capital and still not make a significant impact. We need to plant churches that function together as a body. Thousands of individual churches will not pull down Satan's strongholds. It is only when the parts come together as a co-ordinated whole, only when we rise up as a unified body of Christ in the city, that the church will be seen as a force to be reckoned with.

Merely building "village-type" churches is not the real goal as these are small and parochial by definition. Even if your church grows to 1,000 you won't make much of an impact on your city, as long as you are working in isolation. There are many positive features of smaller churches such as their often strong pastoral ministry and clear local vision. However, the tendency is to become isolated and detached from the overall vision of the Lord in the city or region. 'Village' churches are often found to lack direction when viewed from the perspective of the whole.

The diversity of local churches is only truly valuable if there is unity and co-ordination. The particular function and capabilities of the hand are only useful as part of the body. If you cut the hand off, it will cease to function. No matter how distinctive the diversity is, it is only of value when functioning as part of the whole. That is why we want our Kensington Temple satellite churches to remain a co-ordinated part of the total vision. If 2,000 churches stood together and co-ordinated their efforts in the capital, if we functioned together as the body of Christ in the city, alongside other churches in the city, then we could do something significant for the Lord in London.

That is when we will take the city! We will see Satan's strongholds brought down, even uprooting those demonic dominions that have gone unchallenged for centuries. Institutions will bow the knee to the lordship of Christ and the city will know that God is alive and well in London!

A city church is apostolic

As we have seen, the structure of the city church is drawn straight from the New Testament. Therefore it carries all the characteristics of the early church including its apostolic nature. A city church will be apostolic in three main ways: foundation, leadership and conversion.

Apostolic foundation

The church of Jesus Christ was founded upon the apostles and prophets of the New Testament revelation. This means that the Lord revealed the gospel to the apostles who were eye witnesses of the events. They reported, interpreted and proclaimed these events under the inspiration of the Holy Spirit. Ever since then the true church has been built by the Lord Jesus on this one foundation. If we deviate from it we are not building his church but a human edifice. A city church cannot afford to do that. It may be possible to build a citywide organisation that way, but it will be a false church and not the powerful expression of the body of Christ that God wants to bring about.

Apostolic leadership

The New Testament church was founded upon the teaching of the first generation of living apostles. Now they are no longer with us, and instead we have their authoritative directives recorded for us in Scripture. Does this mean that there is no need for further apostolic leadership today? Far from it. The work of the apostle is necessary until the building is complete. In fact all the ministries of Ephesians 4:11 are necessary until the ministry of the church is completed. We do not need any further revelation of Scripture. But we do need breakthrough ministries that can take the church forward into new levels of maturity. We need those who can bring structure and direction to churches. We need the apostolic anointing for signs and wonders and for raising up the full range of New Testament ministries. We need people of apostolic faith who can penetrate new areas of society and take the gospel into the neglected regions. Above all we need apostolic leaders who can raise up city churches so that we can see a restoration of this level of corporate life and witness today.

Apostolic conversion

We must also see a restoration to the church of full Christian initiation. Much modern conversion to Christ is barely recognisable as New Testament conversion. Many have only a partial Christian experience and stumble through life at a subnormal standard of Christian living. Much Christian teaching and debate on the subject centres on defending the low levels of Christian initiation in the church today and seeking to show that 'we have all got it all anyway.' Rather, we should be seeking to return to standards of conversion that are fully biblical. When people turned to Christ in the New Testament church they were instructed to achieve at least four things which constituted full Christian initiation.

Repentance

Without true repentance there can be no salvation. Repentance is a change of mind and heart which leads to a radical change of lifestyle. If we are not truly repentant and our lives do not change accordingly, how can we honestly confront the sins of our city? How can our hearts throb with the Father's compassion if we are dominated by our selfish desires?

Faith

Faith is the other side of the coin to repentance. One denotes what we forsake, and the other what we embrace. Faith must be real. It includes both believing in the gospel of truth and in the truth of the gospel, who is Jesus Christ. It means that we learn to trust him with everything and for everything. In other words, we are called to a life of faith and not just to a moment of faith designed simply to get our names into heaven's roll book. We will need strong faith if we are going to take the city: the kind of faith that confronts kings and removes the mountains of opposition. We must make sure that it is bred well into every convert and into every disciple of Christ.

Baptism in water

This was the ordinance of initiation into the church. People were added to the church by baptism and the New Testament knows no such thing as an unbaptised disciple. It was more than a witness or a symbol of what had happened to a new believer. It was also a powerful part of the process of coming to Christ. It was how disciples made their public commitment to Christ. Just as Roman soldiers would make a public oath of allegiance when enlisting in the imperial army, so by baptism new believers would publicly own their allegiance to Christ. Baptism was viewed as burial of the old life and the beginning of new life in Christ. It was not a crude means of gaining entrance into heaven, for salvation comes only through faith in Christ. Nevertheless, it is an essential part of discipleship and without baptism, Christian experience is seriously subnormal.

Baptism in the Holy Spirit

The baptism of the Holy Spirit is promised to all believers. It can only be given to believers, but is nonetheless a part of Christian initiation. As it was not automatic, the New Testament church leaders took careful steps to ensure that every new convert received the Holy Spirit. They did this through prayer and the laying on of hands, and the Lord confirmed the experience with speaking in tongues. The gift of the Holy Spirit is essential for us today if we are serious about reaching our cities for God. It was the coming of the Holy Spirit that made all the difference to the first Christians and exactly the same applies today. Without him we are powerless and have nothing to offer the people, but with him we can fulfil God's best plans for any city.

A city church is large

City churches of the New Testament were not small and insignificant groups. Far from it. They were large gatherings of believers who made their presence felt right across the city. People were falling over Christians everywhere! Take thechurch of Jerusalem. Depending on the population of Jerusalem, estimates of which vary, I calculate that the Jerusalem church grew to at least 50,000 within three years.

Just think about what happened on the day of Pentecost. That day the 120 would have grown to at least 5,000 including the women and children who also believed. Despite the fact that the majority of those would have been temporarily in Jerusalem for the feast, the church continued to grow. Shortly afterwards, 5,000 men were added to the faith and this would have had an effect on their families also. Later, the word of God spread and the number of disciples in Jerusalem multiplied greatly, the majority of the priests also coming to Christ. Historians tell us that there could have been up to 20,000 priests in Jerusalem at that time.

When the apostles were brought before the Sanhedrin to be questioned by the high priest, he said,

> *"We gave you strict orders not to teach in this name, yet you have filled Jerusalem with your teaching..."*
>
> *(Acts 5:28)*

Most of the priests were Sadducees and were antagonistic to the gospel, since their doctrine did not allow them to accept the validity of any resurrection, let alone the resurrection of Jesus.

Can you imagine the effect that a breakthrough among this most resistant group in Jerusalem would have had on the rest of the population? When the clergy begin to get saved we're just about ready for revival! This rate of growth continued for many years despite the heavy persecution and the early scattering of the believers recorded in Acts 8:1. Years later the elders of Jerusalem told Paul,

> *"You see, brother, how many thousands of Jews have believed..."*
> *(Acts 21:20)*

The Jerusalem church was not unique in its size. Similar huge urban churches grew in Antioch, Corinth, Ephesus, Rome and in other great cities of the Empire.

When some people see crowded churches they are immediately on the alert. "What's wrong here?" they ask as they sniff the air for the smell of compromise. I object to the idea that churches can only become large through the lowering of Christian standards. Such ideas often betray a meanness of mind and a slim grasp of the greatness of God. Crowds are made up of people: people with needs and potential for the Lord's work. Jesus was moved with compassion when he saw the crowds and longed to shepherd them. Similar compassion for multitudes of lost and lonely people, living their superficial God-estranged lives, should drive us to our knees until we have a strategy and a ministry that will cause people to follow Christ joyfully in their thousands.

Most British churches make a virtue out of smallness. "Small is beautiful," we are told. A recent article in a Christian magazine was cynical and suspicious of megachurches. The view expressed was that large churches were impersonal, lacking in quality commitment, and low on discipleship. They were said to grow by drawing members from other churches. I can only speak for Kensington Temple, but I know we "give away" far more people than we ever "take" from other churches. Many come to us from all over the world not even knowing the Lord personally. They get saved, filled with the Holy Spirit and trained. Then we send them out be effective for God all over the world and in many different kinds of churches. Every year we send out around 1,500 people this way.

It is time for British pastors to move away from maintenance thinking to a mission mentality. We must be kingdom-orientated and not narrow and parochial. Such thinking will never significantly advance the gospel in our cities. London needs not one but many megachurches, where quantity does not spoil quality. The New Testament churches ministered effectively to the needs of individuals and yet had many thousands in their membership.

What about our cities today? A city church in the larger cities could well have hundreds of thousands. It is possible that 50% of the population of Jerusalem found Christ, and in times of revival it is not unknown for the whole population to come to Christ. Think of the effect that would have on your city!

A city church is visible

> *"You are the light of the world. A city on a hill cannot be hidden."*
>
> *(Matthew 5:14)*

In Jerusalem during the time of this revival you could not get away from Christians. In some South American nations today over 20% of the people are believers. Imagine if two out of every ten people that you met on the street were born again, Spirit filled Christians! In these places, if you start preaching on the street corner, dozens of people gather around, and they are the believers encouraging you!

Once in Brazil, while I was delayed in Brasilia airport, I watched a European man react as various Christians approached him and handed him literature. As soon as he discarded one leaflet, someone else handed him another. He couldn't get away from the witness and testimony - there were Christians everywhere! He had not seen anything like it in Europe.

However, size is not the only factor in visibility. It takes co-ordinated action. There could be two million believers in London, but if they did not move together as a body, they would probably go unnoticed. Jesus said that people do not leave a lighted lamp under a bowl. Instead they put it on a stand and it gives light to everyone in the house.

> *"In the same way, let your light shine before men, that they may see your good deeds and praise your Father in heaven."*
> *(Matthew 5:16).*

As we work together, the light of our good works, social action, evangelism and moral strength must shine out brilliantly in the midst of London's darkness.

For decades the British media have been marginalising Bible believing Christians as fanatics on the fringe of Christianity. Imagine the shock waves that will sweep through the UK when the media wake up to the realisation that the evangelical church in Great Britain is not just some group on the fringes but represents mainstream Christianity. They are already beginning to sit up and take notice. There has been a surge of media interest in the evangelical position, focussing on its rapid growth and popularity, particularly among charismatics. They are realising that there is something "big" going on.

A city church is powerful

The Jerusalem church was certainly full of spiritual power. There are four aspects of that power seen in Acts 4.

Intercession

The churches of Acts were powerful centres of prayer. Whenever there was a need of any kind, the church prayed. The power of prayer was clearly demonstrated in Acts 4, after the release of Peter and John. They had been bound over by a high court ruling that sought to prevent them from continuing to preach the gospel. However, it was their fixed intention to obey God rather than this ruling, even though it was made by the Sanhedrin, the highest court in the land for the Jews, and the very body that had condemned Jesus to death not many months before.

All this called for prayer. But it was prayer with a difference. There was no time to send out a prayer letter or wait for the weekly prayer meeting. The believers gathered for emergency prayer and it was no polite tea and cake occasion! Powerful effective prayer rose to the throne as they all lifted their voices in a great concert of prayer.

Their praying arose out of a powerful move of God. It came from people who were totally committed to the cause of Christ in Jerusalem. The kind of answer God gave would determine the course of the gospel in that city and beyond. The believers were at the very centre of things, caught up in the vortex of the purposes of God. The spiritual destiny of the city of Jerusalem was being prayed out in that room, as believer linked to believer, pleading their case according to the will of God. They called, not for their own safety or security, but only for God to be glorified. They were desperate for the Lord to come and vindicate himself and to show the power of the name of Jesus in the city. They asked for boldness and God heard them.

> *After they prayed, the place where they were meeting was shaken. And they were all filled with the Holy Spirit and spoke the word of God boldly.*
>
> (Acts 4:31)

A city church will pray like that. The people will pray strategically and with a sense of destiny. How God answers will determine the course of the kingdom of God not only in that city, but beyond, in the entire nation and even further afield. The city church will pray with great corporate authority. Jesus' teaching on the two or three gathered together in his name was not an expression of his preference for small prayer meetings but a revelation of the spiritual principle of agreement.

> *I tell you that if two of you on earth agree about anything you ask for, it will be done for you by my Father in heaven.*
>
> (Matthew 18:19)

The Lord was showing the power of praying in agreement. If it takes only two agreeing on what is permitted and forbidden in heaven in order to see it birthed through prayer on earth, imagine the power in thousands coming together in agreement. What would happen if whole churches were to stand together, and with one voice cry out to the Lord concerning issues of citywide significance? To pray like this requires real heart level unity. It means joining together with common vision and common purpose. A citywide network of our churches and ministries standing together in agreement, such as we propose, could take any city for Christ.

Spiritual warfare

The same is true of spiritual warfare. The believers meeting for prayer after the release of Peter and John knew that they were in a spiritual war, that God had his enemies. They quoted Psalm 2, which goes on to declare God's glorious victory,

> *"The One enthroned in heaven laughs; the Lord scoffs at them. Then he rebukes them in his anger and terrifies them in his wrath..."*
>
> (Psalm 2:4-5)

In spiritual warfare,when you have that many people moving together in unity, God releases a powerful anointing that breaks the yoke.

> *How good and pleasant it is when brothers live together in unity... For there the Lord bestows his blessing, even life forevermore.*
>
> (Psalm 133:1,3)

When a whole stream, a whole movement of churches which saturates the city, begins to move and act together, the powers of Satan come tumbling down, releasing institutions which have been long gripped by principalities and powers. Christ will be glorified in the arts, the media, business, commerce, industry, education, medicine and politics. When the influences of the powers of darkness are pushed back, the heavens open and revival breaks out. This is true spiritual victory.

For too long, spiritual warfare has amounted to little more than taking pot shots at the devil! Guerrilla warfare in not enough. We need strategies for out and out war. It is time to stop taking it lying down. Satan has had it practically all his way for long enough and it is time for the church to rise up and take authority over his rebellious and illegal dominion. A city church can be just such a match for Satan. Born in a powerful move of the Spirit, it can grow into a finely-tuned fighting machine that can menace the devil, loose his grip over the city and drive out his demonic hordes. In such an environment people flock to Christ, free from the satanic strongholds that assail the minds of unbelievers, preventing them from hearing and receiving Christ's message. Such a church can move forward and take new ground for the kingdom.

The benefits of this are plain for all to see and enjoy. Every spiritual advance benefits the whole body of Christ. Vested interests alone should be reason enough for every church in the city to rejoice over the progress of churches with a citywide influence. This is far better than feeling intimidated or overshadowed by the success of larger churches.

Boldness

The key note of the Acts 4 prayer meeting was boldness. Powerful manifestation of the Holy Spirit brings boldness. When a city church begins to rise and stand for Christ in the city, the same boldness comes on everybody.

When I was a new believer, I was taken to Tower Hill in London, to witness. I felt I was going to go to the Tower to have my head cut off! I was so frightened that I stood at the back tying to look inconspicuous. Then the hecklers came, hurling their abuse. After a while I forgot my timidity and was ready to go for them, in love of course! That was my Jesus they were talking about. Individually we are easy prey, but when we stand with each other we will be as bold as lions.

We should not be perceived as a negligible minority. So often the church's voice is the last to be heard, and the fault does not always lie with our opponents. Much of the church is held down by a spirit of timidity. Courage and boldness is often lacking. We need to stand up and be counted. We must make Christ's voice heard in every place, every situation, and every corner of our urban communities.

A new dynamic enters when you are part of a growing city church. You feel part of the winning team! You are an ambassador for Christ and you don't need to back down before anyone. The world will stop laughing and begin once again to fear the Church, not just for the sheer size of its numbers nor because of its growth, but for the spiritual authority that it possesses.

The miraculous

The prayer of Acts 4 arose out of a crisis in the Jerusalem church. However, the challenge was not directed to man, but to God. Neither councils, government authorities, nor voices that oppose the plan of God have the last word, no matter how aggressively they speak. God's power is supreme. He answers with a torrent of supernatural power. City churches are called to fight big battles, often in the public arena where religions, ideologies and politics oppose the claims of Christ. God overthrows the opposition every time. Just when the enemy appears to have played his master stroke, God comes through with a miracle. The Jewish authorities couldn't deny the healing of the lame man. They tried to stop the preaching, but they could not stop the signs and wonders which confirmed its power and truth.

The disciples in Jerusalem knew the place of signs and wonders and were not hesitant in asking for them.

> *"Stretch out your hand to heal and perform miraculous signs and wonders through the name of your holy servant Jesus."*
>
> *(Acts 4:30)*

The Lord was not reluctant to answer. The issues were too great. God always shows his power at crucial moments of destiny.

> *With great power the apostles continued to testify to the resurrection of the Lord Jesus, and much grace was upon them all.*
>
> *(Acts 4:33)*

Things have not changed since those early days in Jerusalem. The issues remain the same. Men in authority still oppose the gospel. They want to gag the church, but just give the Lord a united body, willing to grapple with the larger spiritual issues of a city, and watch him move. He will release the full flood of his power if we line up with his great plans. He will come through with the overflow of his supernatural grace and shake our cities with the manifestation of his miracle working power.

A city church is resourceful

When a church reaches citywide proportions there is almost no limit to the kind of activity it can engage in. It can successfully run large scale social ministries, educational programmes, Bible colleges and mission activities. In short, all the kinds of activities that are usually only possible for a whole denomination to engage in can now operate from the city church itself. As a result, a new dynamic enters these programmes. The work is much closer to grass roots, and people's ministry, vision and calling can be put into practice right where they are, or for those with a translocal call, released from the city church base.

Faith for finances

City churches can also make big breakthroughs in terms of finance. Once more I am on dangerous ground, according to many British church leaders. However, finance as a subject is not to be ignored. If Christians really are going to push ahead in this vision for society they must throw off forever false views of money. It is true that your spirituality is not to be measured by the amount you have in your bank account - either by how much you have or how little you have. Being poor or rich does not mean that you are more or less spiritual. But money is needed for God's work today. Big city churches have the capacity to move against the strongholds of money - both the lack of it and the love of it.

People resources

Because of its size, a city church is also packed with people resources. If the entire focus of the church is on equipping the people for ministry, a city church can effectively mobilise. There is a place for everyone's ministry. As soon as new ministries emerge, there are outlets immediately available. In the context of church planting and expansion there is no limit to the opportunities available.

The initial success of the new house churches was partly due to transfer growth, although they are now also effective in evangelism. The very reason they originally attracted members from other churches was that people were tired of directionless church life. Much church life was like going on the same merry-go-round and getting nowhere. Very few churches were effectively mobilising their members. Major ministries in the body of Christ were being neglected. There was very little prophetic input and no apostolic foundation, and as a result people were often disheartened and many churches atrophied.

In the 1970's a new release of apostolic ministries occurred in the new churches and there was a massive move towards them. People felt fathered, protected and secure. When the prophetic ministries began speaking, people found direction; they began to know where they were going.

A real confidence comes into a church which knows that it is hearing from the Lord and has a clear vision to fulfil. A sense of celebration and victory springs up. That is why we need all the ministries of Christ to be released in the Church. No individual ministry on its own can fully express the ministry of Christ, but when all the ministry gifts of Christ are operating together, the full impact of Christ's ministry, in and through a church, is felt far and wide. When the evangelists are anointed, people come to Christ in their hundreds. Through those truly called to the pastoral and teaching ministries, new believers are nurtured and properly founded in the things of God. The people grow and become strong. A city church will have all these ministries functioning fully and freely, successfully modelling them for others who will also rise up in these gifts of the Holy Spirit. And they are available throughout the entire city church structure. Each individual unit, no matter how small, has the same apostolic foundation, the same level of prophetic direction, and the same access to all the other ministries successfully operating in the main church.

A city church is organised

Many people shy away from anything to do with organisation, calling it "anti-charismatic". They say the Church is an organism rather than an organisation and that we simply have to obey the prompting of the Spirit at all times in order to find our rightful place in the body. While this is partially true, we must remember that the Holy Spirit does reveal patterns of organisation for him to work through. In fact, the very image of the body, used by the apostle Paul, shows just how important the right kind of organisation is.

How long would the human body survive if the members were not organised into a co-ordinated whole? Of course what matters most is that the members of the body are arranged as God intends them to be, because they must be organised in order to function as a co-ordinated whole.

Flexible structures

To build a church that can influence our cities for God, we urgently need to develop the right structures. At all cost we must avoid the imposition of rigid regulations that bind and control, but we do need free and flexible structures to promote growth. That is the point of the parable of the wineskins. The old wineskins which represented the Judaism of Jesus' day had lost their flexibility and could not contain the new wine of the Kingdom of God. New wine needs new wineskins that are flexible enough to receive the dynamic life of God.

Structures must serve us, not control us. No structure can produce life or fruit of itself. Take, for example, a grapevine growing up a trellis. The trellis has no life in itself. The life is in the vine but it needs the structure to hold it up and allow it to take shape. You cannot produce life by structure. Just as the vine does not owe its life to the trellis that supports it, so the life of a city church does not have its source in any structure. Our life comes from Christ and nowhere else.

> *So then, just as you received Christ Jesus as Lord, continue to live in him, [7]rooted and built up in him, strengthened in the faith as you were taught, and overflowing with thankfulness.*
> (*Colossians 2:6-7*)

For us at Kensington Temple, the need for appropriate structures is made all the more urgent due to the degree of growth we are experiencing. Unless we are careful, our structures soon lose their ability to cope with the level of growth the Lord is giving. We must be able not only to sustain the present growth but also to handle the even greater levels ahead. As the disciples found out, it is possible to have such an unusual catch of fish that your nets break!

One church: many churches

Everything we have seen so far about a city church affirms that it is not just a loose collection of congregations but is effectively organised at many different levels. Each individual part is not only a valid unit, itself fully functioning according to its unique gift and call, but also a co-ordinated part of the whole. Every level of the Holy Spirit's activity finds its own valid expression. This expression ranges from the macro to the micro, from great celebrations of the whole body, to intimate gatherings for table fellowship in homes.

The Jerusalem church in Acts was highly organised. There was a clear structure that provided leadership, membership and the exercise of spiritual gifts and ministries. There is no way that such a large number of new believers could have been successfully discipled and integrated into the main body of the church without good organisation. The Jerusalem church was structured to ensure that every function of church life was catered for at every level.

In particular, the organisation of a city church must provide for multi-level fellowship and ministry. Only then can the various parts function as a co-ordinated whole. This is where the effectiveness of a city church comes from, as we can accomplish far more working together than we could ever do on our own. How many functions of the total body do you think a hand could perform on its own? In a city church, all the churches and ministries are organised so that they function as a body, with one mind and one spirit pursuing the same vision.

All this is based on relationship and unity of purpose, not on institutional directives. A city church will not rely on regulations to get results. Unity and co-operation is voluntary. It grows naturally out of a relationship with the Holy Spirit as he gives the same vision to those who are sensitive to what he is doing in the city. It also grows out of the corporate vision which holds the parts together. The churches that are linked to the city church network are both independent wholes and interdependent parts. The city church is both one church working as a body and many churches working as equally valid expressions of the body of Christ in their area.

A city church is multicultural

A city church is ideally suited for the flexibility necessary to cope with different cultural and racial mixes. In recent years church growth analysts have highlighted an important principle of growth. They call it the homogeneous principle. More than 70% of churches that are growing are monocultural, that is, they have one main culture. This is a good principle of ministry as we are most probably able to reach people like ourselves. Churches flourish along lines of common social and cultural affinity.

The homogeneous principle can be seen in Acts. The Greek-speaking Jews who came to Christ in Jerusalem received ministry as a cultural group from their own kind, with the backing of the apostles (Acts 6:1-7).

But homogeneity is not all there is to church life. Though we are different members we are in fact united in one body. We need to have a church that expresses the many cultures present in a city as this ensures that no culture is excluded from the gospel. They can all find valid expression in a city church. At Kensington Temple we uphold a multicultural type of worship, all coming together for big celebrations to express our unity. At the same time those of different nationalities and cultures fellowship in the various ethnic churches and sub-groups of the church, where they can begin to give fuller expression to their own cultural distinctives. This does not weaken our unity in Christ, but strengthens it as the distinctives of language and culture are given room to flourish within the larger life of the body.

This method is effective both for evangelism and pastoral care as language barriers are lifted, freeing the groups to reach out and care for those in their own culture and community. There is nothing quite like being able to praise God, receive teaching and express yourself in your own language, and to find others with whom you can do it is a real blessing, especially if you are in a foreign land. There are other less obvious cultural expressions that are just as real as language - food, for example! Any meal in

Kensington Temple, with its 110 different nationalities, can easily be a gastronomic gallop around the world! We have learned not to underestimate the importance of cultural differences in the kingdom of God. Of course the culture of heaven is dominant, but it is surprising how enriching it is when the kingdom of God is allowed to be freely expressed through the diverse cultures of city life.

No church today can afford to ignore the multicultural elements of the city. This will have to lead to a deliberate attempt to reach out across cultural barriers ministering to others unlike ourselves. After all, if we are called to make disciples of all nations, why not start on our doorstep? The whole world comes to London, and the same dynamic is present in most cities today. We have found that our multicultural philosophy of church brings a great blessing, as it satisfies the heart of God which is for all peoples. It is like a foretaste of heaven when the nations worship him as members of the one body. We have also found that it helps us remain mission conscious. Many have received a call to go to some part of the world to help in social relief or to preach the gospel as a result of crosscultural contact made in the multicultural setting of our church in London.

A city church is effective

The final characteristic of a city church summarises all the rest. City churches are, by definition, effective. They are effective in evangelism and social action. They are effective in pastoral care and discipleship. In short they are effective in functioning as God's agent in the world, the body of Christ on earth. Here I am not just speaking about the outward signs of success but about true effectiveness in the work of the kingdom of God.

Evangelism flourishes as the church is flung headlong into expansive mission, influence soon reaching international dimensions. City churches have the resources, the anointing, and the ministry to work effectively on a large scale. They have the potential to bring social and political changes that can affect the whole city and even the moral and spiritual climate of the nation.

Think about all that is being achieved by the Marches for Jesus which began in London in the mid 1980's. The media try to play them down, but as they happen again and again and grow bigger and bigger, television, radio and newspapers are not able to disregard them. The traffic is stopped and people ask, "What is this demonstration all about?" But it's neither a demonstration, nor a political protest, it is the Church on the march in praise of the Lord Jesus Christ. The same dynamic is released through a city church.

Many people are beginning to fear and vehemently oppose the Church's power to exert social and political influence. But we must be effective agents of change in our society. If we do not make the changes, others will, without sympathy for our agenda. Unless we act, the days will come when their influence will dominate and we will cry out to God for precisely what we can now achieve in him. That is, effective churches exercising a powerful ministry across entire metropolitan areas.

Each of these characteristics of a city church belong to it as a whole rather than as individual congregations. The key is found in churches and ministries functioning as a network. All the parts must function together as a co-ordinated whole.

7

THE KENSINGTON TEMPLE CITY CHURCH

We have a vision to become a fully functioning city church by the end of the decade, with all the characteristics I have been describing in place. For this to happen, I believe that the central church must grow to at least 30,000 people, and we must plant 2,000 satellite churches across the city.

The structure

From the beginning it was always our intention to be one church, and not to plant separate self-existent churches unconnected to the main body. We are not all doing separate things in our own little corners but are standing together in God's work. We are partners together, building a city church; the satellite churches have a function that cannot be performed by the central body, and vice versa. So, we have a two-fold need, to function both as independent wholes and as interdependent parts. This is where the city church concept is so helpful.

Our overall church structure consists of a central body with many satellite bodies in orbit. This model, which was put forward a number of years ago by Wynne Lewis, the former Senior Pastor, is ideally suited to fulfil the vision. In some churches the term "satellite church" is used of smaller sub-divisions of the one central congregation which never function fully as churches in their own right. We do not follow that system. Rather, we encourage our satellite groups to grow and develop so that they develop as fully functioning churches while also remaining a part of the overall structure. Therefore, we are both one church and many churches, exactly as the city church model suggests.

This pattern can be illustrated from the solar system. The planets are fully-functioning systems even though they are revolving around the sun. Can you imagine the earth breaking free from its connection to the sun? It is the precise orbit of the earth around the sun that gives it the ability to sustain life. Therefore, our satellite churches are parts of the larger whole without losing their integrity or identity as churches in their own right.

There are two forces which operate on a satellite body. Both of these dynamics must operate, and both must maintain the satellite balance. In a city church, both principles must be owned, verbalised and held in constant balance. I call these forces the *pull away* from and the *pull towards* the central body. It is these two forces operating in tension that maintain the orbit.

Both of these dynamics are positive and must be encouraged to operate freely. The *pull towards* is the attraction of the central church, bringing people into the centre to be trained and equipped. The *pull away* is the effective force that takes them out again into the world to put into practice what they have learned. The central church must encourage the *pull away* to take place. Satellites are usually launched by putting a bomb under them! Once in orbit, satellite churches should find out how they can continue to link with and feed back into the central base church.

These two dynamics must therefore be equally operating in both the central church and all its satellites. The central body encourages people in the central church to move out of their complacency and selfishness. The result is that many new churches will be planted and existing satellite churches built up. The satellite bodies also encourage the *pull towards* the centre otherwise the satellite will become unnecessarily isolated and less effective. Anything less than this will not achieve the vision of a city church. The right balance between the two forces keeps the satellites in orbit. It should not be seen as bondage, but something that gives life and liberty as in the analogy of the earth and the sun.

The *pull away* from the central church

Having seen the basic structure of the Kensington Temple satellite model, let us look first at the *pull away*: how it works and how we facilitate it.

The great commission

Part of the *pull away* is in obedience to Matthew 28:19 in which the Lord commands us to go and make disciples of all nations. The central meetings, whatever else they achieve, must motivate and inspire people to step out in obedience to the great commission. The vast reserve of people resources must be trained, equipped and sent out into ministry. We make sure that people don't just listen to the testimonies of others who are doing it but begin to go out and do it themselves. This approach is in line with the usual trend in large inner city churches, especially in London. Every three years 70% of our congregation changes, but they leave saved, filled with the Holy Spirit and equipped to reach out with the gospel.

We co-operate with this trend and actively seek to thrust people out in the work in obedience to the Lord's command. Some years ago when I took over our Sunday night meeting I prayed that many hundreds would leave trained and envisioned to start a work for Jesus. I preached accordingly, verbalising my desires before the people. The concern of some was whether those who moved on into ministries outside the main services would be replaced, but the Lord honoured what we did. After one year more than 20% of the church was involved in the satellite programme alone, and the Sunday evening attendance had doubled, from 500 to over 1,000. The more you give away, the more God gives back to you. Do not worry about giving your people away. Rather, send them out to make disciples. By now many people in our churches ought to be teachers instead of sitting in a row listening to elementary principles over and over again. We should be constantly launching people into leadership and ministry.

Equipping and releasing

Ephesians 4:11-12 explains the reason why Christ gave leadership ministries to the Church. These ministry gifts exist to equip and deploy the members of the Church into the work of the Church. Usually, there is only time for one message to be preached at each meeting and therefore room for only one preacher. Everyone who is out preaching in our satellite churches is exercising a gift that would otherwise be dormant, but is now active. This *pull away* ensures that every ministry God has given can find expression and be developed. There are many people who are currently in the main body whom I am hoping will obey God's call and either launch into orbit with more new satellites, take up their place in the arena of world missions, or find some other sphere of meaningful service for Christ.

Fruitfulness

Another *pull away* is the desire to reproduce after your own kind. That is fruitfulness. If there is any valid move of God in the church, it is there because it was birthed through some God-given ministry. This is something worth reproducing. What you are excited about you will want to share with others. This is the principle of spiritual reproduction. People should be so excited to be part of a genuine move of God that they want to see it spread right across the city. They should not just sit back enjoying it month after month and year after year.

Reaching local people

The *pull away* focuses on local needs. There are people in our local streets, blocks and boroughs who have needs that are not being met by our central church or by anybody else, and they will not be met if we are only to be found worshipping comfortably in our regular meetings. It will only happen when people get involved in outreach projects, fellowship groups and church planting programmes. There are many thousands of needy people living in London's vast spiritual wasteland. We cannot keep what we have to ourselves but must reach out with an effective ministry which is relevant to people as and where they are.

Sociological factors

There is a great need for smaller congregational fellowships. People can tire of only attending large services. After a while they want something a little more interactive, they want to get to know the people in the church, and to be known so that they can pray for each other. We have sought to solve this problem in the way we structure our church.

A church of 25 to 175 people lends itself well to congregational worship, but in any gathering above that number a celebration dynamic takes over. It becomes impossible to know everybody well. It is easy to get lost in the crowd. That may be fine for a while, but the Holy Spirit will soon open you up to some more meaningful type of fellowship. This is another aspect of the *pull away*. It would be relatively easy to come to Kensington Temple for two years and yet not really get to know anyone, if you were only a part of the larger celebration and teaching meetings. This could give the impression that it is not a caring church, and this is not the case. That is where our power cell and satellite church programmes come into their own. I will say more about these in chapter eight.

Logistical factors

Finally, there are practical considerations such as transport and distance, and many other logistical factors that can be part of the *pull away*. These prompt us to get more involved in de-centralised aspects of church life.

All of these factors act as valid contributors to the *pull away* from the central body. We all recognise that London will not be won if we simply take the blessing freely flowing in the central church programme without moving on from what we learn there. Therefore, we accept the challenges of the *pull away* and help our people to step out, in line with the vision.

The *pull towards* the main church

Having seen how the *pull away* operates in the church, what now is the point of the *pull towards* the central meetings? Everyone sees the need for the central church programme as a means for attracting people into the church, but how does this need apply to people who have been saved and equipped to launch out into the de-centralised ministries of the church? Why do we encourage links to be maintained with the central church after we have moved forward in frontline ministries? There are many people who have come to Christ in the satellite churches who were never in the central church to begin with. Of what relevance is the central church to them?

Before I deal with these issues in more detail, let me stress right away that the *pull towards* is just as vital to the Kensington Temple vision as the *pull away.* If this dynamic did not operate the whole vision would collapse. The *pull towards* serves to maintain the continuing partnership in fulfilling the vision to reach London with the gospel. It also ensures that the central church is not depleted, but is replenished. If we want the tree to continue to bear fruit we cannot let the root die. There must be feedback into the central church or else the root will no longer be there to support the branch. So, what is the *pull towards* the central church?

The overall vision

The vision does not belong to the central church alone. It must be owned and carried by every part, even in the decentralised churches and ministries. The vision will keep us all together, sharing the work-load, rather than carrying on with our own ministry concerns, leaving the central church to carry all the weight. As with the Jews of Haggai's day, when everyone was preoccupied with their own goals, they neglected God's greater plans for the city.

> *"You expected much, but see, it turned out to be little. What you brought home, I blew away. Why?" declares the LORD Almighty. "Because of my house, which remains a ruin, while each of you is busy with his own house."*
>
> *(Haggai 1:9)*

The larger vision is to build the house of the Lord in the city and this demands that we safeguard against getting side-tracked in things of lesser importance. The central thrust must not be lost but consistently turned outwards into the city. The *pull towards* ensures that this happens.

All this must not be seen as selfish holding on by leaders of the central church. Rather, it involves giving the vision away so that others can run with it and see it fulfilled. The vision must be reproduced zonally in boroughs. I can even see it being outworked in smaller areas such as wards, housing estates or even streets. We could never reach our target of 2,000 churches simply by sending people out to plant churches. No matter how well we managed them and cared for them it would not fulfil the vision. By that method we would achieve no more than 200, or ten per cent of the goal. However, if all the Kensington Temple churches fully adopt the vision we could certainly do it. We would then be working together, the stronger congregations encouraging the weaker ones and the more successful sharing their insights with those that are not yet developing.

A centre of celebration and excellence

The main church serves as a centre of celebration and excellence. It's good to be part of it! In the past some satellite leaders have feared the pull of the main church and have tried to play down their connection with it in front of their members. Without exception, as I have studied this for five or six years, I have noticed how every satellite church that has stopped talking about its links with Kensington Temple has suffered a negative effect on its life and growth. It is almost like cutting off the feeder line or like saying, "I'm not part of that family, I don't need them". This is totally false strategy, and the end result is sterility. What then are the specific elements or qualities in the central church that make it good to maintain the relationship and the links?

Apostolic and prophetic ministry

First, there is the apostolic and prophetic ministry of the central church. There is no doubt that the Lord has raised us up as an apostolic and prophetic church in the city. This ensures that there is a good foundation and direction for the whole structure. If our churches and ministries remain part of our structure then they have something firm on which to build. We are also blessed by many other leading national and international ministries that come offering significant input and keep us in touch with what the Holy Spirit is doing all over the world.

Training

There are also the training resources of the central church. We are developing at a tremendous rate, with new programmes and resources coming on line all the time. The training grows out of the vision and is tailored exactly to the needs of the many ministries God has called from our ranks.

Accountability

Finally, there is the matter of accountability - both legal and spiritual covering. Those who are not accountable don't count in the kingdom. It is as simple as that. Even if you had a church of 10,000, and you yourself were not accountable, you could have no confidence in what you have built. God looks at the foundations. He wants spiritual churches, accountable to spiritual authority. It is imperative that everything be done in order and this carries legal as well as spiritual responsibilities. Every satellite church is under the covering of Kensington Temple and we are responsible for them, which is why there must be accountability.

I have had to learn the principle of spiritual authority. Sometimes it has been very hard for me to submit in spiritual matters. At times it has felt like bondage, but in the end it has always brought freedom. I am absolutely convinced that I would not have been entrusted with the degree of responsibility and spiritual authority I have now if I had not learned some hard lessons in the school of submission. You first have to serve before you can lead. You may have to learn to carry someone else's vision faithfully before the Lord will allow you one of your own. I have proved it time and time again. True submission always pays. If you sow submission, you reap authority.

So if you, as a leader, want to do your own thing and think the people in your church don't need spiritual covering, you are fooled. Your people are unprotected unless you yourself are in submission. I am not talking about "heavy" shepherding; we want flexibility; we don't want people to be controlled and under anyone's thumb. But this spiritual principle of submission to authority before being given authority is after all a joyful thing, since being under authority yourself releases you in authority and provides the covering needed to function freely in your anointing. This is what the central church and its leadership provide.

Positive feedback

A few years ago, God gave us a challenge. He led us to look at our entire church programme and evaluate its effectiveness, especially in the light of some new financial constraints that were becoming apparent. It is remarkable how financial challenges focus the mind. We examined in particular the training and the satellite church planting programmes. It seemed that the more we did, the less we were able to do. We had an advanced discipleship and apprenticeship training scheme called the Joshua Programme which was heavily supported out of central funds. We started off with three Joshuas, then five, then ten and finally we had twelve. Then we broke the bank! We could do no more because we had reached the end of our resources. The next year we wanted 24 Joshuas and did not feel we could say glibly, "God will provide." After some painful heart-searching we came to the conclusion that we were going about it the wrong way. The principle was marvellous: on-the-job training for those moving into full-time Christian work in the Church. But we could not carry it on in that form. Now the Joshua principle has been extended to all who train with us and not restricted just to a few. Now we can have as many students as we like, because they are studying and working part time to pay their own way and so the more we train the more we are able to train.

This same principle can be applied to many different programmes. Ideally it should apply to all. The more we do, the more we should be enabled to do, and the only way that can happen is through positive feedback. We encourage people to plough back into the central church what they have received out of it. It means that we operate according to the principle of sowing and reaping. As we sow seeds and they produce a harvest, we can partake of the harvest and are able to sow even more. This is how a farmer develops his farm. He may start off with a small piece of ground and a small harvest, but he keeps back some of his harvest in order to sow more, enabling him to reap a greater harvest the following year, and so on. This principle can be applied in many different ways. We encourage people to give back to the central church their time, their talents and the experience that they have gained, particularly when they have moved out in some ministry.

The feedback principle is one of the most positive *pull towards* of them all. We have found this to be especially true in our church planting programme. As new churches grow and develop, they begin to put financial resources back into the central church planting ministry, enabling more churches to be planted. It stands to reason also that the greatest levels of expertise in the area of church planting exist in the churches that have been planted out by the central church. The satellite church leaders are among the most knowledgeable in the nation when it comes to planting urban churches. This is because they are doing it, and doing it well. Many do not yet know themselves how much they have to offer, but we are seeking to make full use of them in our training programmes. Increasingly, they are the main teachers in our regular church planting and church growth seminars.

The *pull towards,* then, involves placing back into the central body resources, prayer, energy, co-operation, co-ordination and indeed finance, so that the central church can push forward even further towards the fulfilment of the vision. It is one of our most important principles of growth.

Let's celebrate!

The dynamic of the celebration meetings is essential to the city church concept. The body must come together; there must be that level of corporate expression. It is a reminder that we are part of the larger whole. We come together to renew our sense of belonging and to affirm our corporate identity. The first central celebration meeting in March 1992 was an enlightening occasion. Faces beamed with joy as over 3,000 people crowded into Westminster Chapel. They seemed to be saying to themselves, "So this is KT!" It was not the whole church, but nevertheless the largest number from our church that had gathered together on any one occasion so far. They were looking around at each other, recognising their friends and fellow-worshippers; so many familiar faces and some not so familiar!

Despite the success of the earlier smaller celebration meetings, no-one anticipated what it would be like when we held our first celebration for the whole Kensington Temple family at the Royal Albert Hall. I will never forget the moment I stood at the podium in that great auditorium to open the evening. We had spent months in preparation and now at last everything was in place. The newly-formed celebration choir, radiant in reds, greens and yellows, had sung their opening piece. The hall was packed to near capacity. Final moments of intercession, sealing many days of prayer and fasting, gave way to excited, expectancy. There was no crowd-pulling performer or visiting preacher: Jesus was centre stage. Everyone's eyes were on him. We had come not in the name of a ministry or an organisation but only to glorify Christ and to celebrate him. The worship songs appropriately rung out from the congregation. "We have a vision for this nation" and "Jesus we celebrate your victory!"

Sensing the strategic importance of the evening, I had carefully prepared in advance my opening words:

"When the day comes that a single church can take and fill a building like the Royal Albert Hall for one of its own meetings, then a new day begins for the British Church. Friends, I declare to you that the new day has begun!"

Knowing that this was probably the largest gathering of any single church in recent British history, I went on boldly to proclaim,

"Let the unseen principalities and powers over this city, let the public officials, let the private citizens and the whole nation know: the Church of Jesus Christ is not dead - we are alive and well! The day of smallness is over. The day of isolationism is ended. From now on we hold the public arena, and this city cannot be the same!"

Then I read a powerful proclamation of the lordship of Christ declaring his truth over the city. It was greeted by prolonged shouts of exultation and triumph as everyone in that place acknowledged and applauded the name of Jesus!

That celebration on 11 November 1992 was nothing less than a festival of sheer joy and a wonderful spiritual party. It demonstrated to us all the value of large scale celebration meetings. They are a potent part of our vision. Without them, there would be no single meeting in Kensington Temple that brings all the central congregations together, let alone all the satellite congregations. We have six central services on a Sunday with the vast majority of people attending only once. Many thousands of people pass through the doors each week and thousands more are scattered all across London. When we come together for the celebration meetings we hear the voice of the Lord together.

Whatever he says to us prophetically is birthed in everybody present, and we can move on as one body with that revelation and direction. And so we continue to grow as we move forward together with one heart and one purpose.

There is a strength that comes from meeting with our brothers and sisters in large numbers. Suddenly we appreciate that we are part of something big. Things are happening! We are not just a tiny minority but a growing movement and part of a worldwide outpouring of the Holy Spirit. We gain a sense of spiritual solidarity. We feel this not just for the present generation, but in a strange way we feel in touch with our history, as we stand in line with the many millions who have gone before us. They were faithful in their generation; we will be faithful in ours. There is also a sense of anticipation, as we experience a tiny foretaste of the future, when we shall stand with the whole company of the redeemed from every generation, race and language, and worship our beloved Saviour for ever! John's revelation of heaven is made all the more real to us,

> *After this I looked and there before me was a great multitude that no-one could count, from every nation, tribe, people and language, standing before the throne and in front of the Lamb. They were wearing white robes and were holding palm branches in their hands. [10]And they cried out in a loud voice: "Salvation belongs to our God, who sits on the throne, and to the Lamb."*
>
> *(Revelation 7:9,10)*

However, the celebrations are not just for inspiration. They are also powerful occasions of spiritual encounter. The level of faith and spiritual manifestation is often far higher than in other meetings. This is partly due to increased levels of expectancy created by the event itself, but also because the whole body is assembled together. The Lord can speak and move freely among his people. The outpouring of his Spirit is often for equipping and the release of ministries. The celebrations are significant times of empowering and commission and are also powerful occasions of prayer and intercession.

With the whole church assembled together, spiritual warfare enters a different level. There are certain things that an army cannot do until every battalion is together in place. Similarly, certain levels of spiritual warfare cannot be entered until the whole church is present for battle. The celebration meetings pose a significant threat to the powers of darkness, which is why we cover them with high levels of prayer and intercession. Our intercessors pray for the events for weeks in advance and they have had to pray against hindrances to the meetings including bomb attacks and extreme traffic congestion. One large meeting in London, which we were involved in, was very nearly ruined because of extraordinary traffic conditions. Many hundreds never even made it to the meeting and turned back after hours of waiting in traffic queues. Later on, we discovered that there were five major happenings in London that evening which caused the traffic to stand still. The combination of these things was surely not coincidental; it was spiritual, but, in spite of this, the meeting was a great success with attendance not significantly below expectations. There would not have been enough room if everyone had turned up!

If the celebrations are significant times of warfare then they are also great opportunities for witness. The testimony of so many Christians getting excited about Jesus is enough for many non-Christians to be attracted to the meetings. When they see us lost in worship and so obviously delighted by the Lord's presence they say, "We want him too." Christians, confident in the event itself, are more inclined to ask friends who don't know Jesus to come to the celebrations. Of course the music and the venue often make the event much more attractive than regular church services and few refuse the opportunity to come.

In the future we will be holding regular celebrations of 10,000 people and more. There will also be joint celebrations with other church groups which will have to be held in football stadia, and there will come a time when there will not be an auditorium in London large enough for what God is doing. So help us by praying for the solution now!

PART THREE

MOBILISATION

8

GETTING INVOLVED!

Mobilisation of the Spirit

It is one thing to have a vision, but quite another matter to see it fulfilled. To bring vision into reality takes time, effort and commitment; it means a single-minded dedication and unrelenting persistence, never giving up until everything is established. Someone has wisely said, "Happy are those who dream dreams and are willing to pay the price to make them come true!" Many Christian leaders have great dreams and wonderful, God-given aspirations, but it seems that few really take hold of the things God has said and battle through until everything is accomplished.

No doubt there are reasons for this. For some, it is the lack of a truly militant attitude towards spiritual things. Jesus said that the kingdom of heaven comes violently and violent men lay hold of it (Matthew 11:12). You have to battle before you can build. King David had first to subdue the enemies of Israel, bringing peace to the nation, before his son Solomon could build the temple and the nation's infrastructure. If you underestimate the strength of the enemy and the intensity of the battle you will never build what God calls you to build.

However, there is a more common failure on the part of leaders, and this one fact accounts for almost all the unfulfilled vision in Christian ministry today. It is the failure to train and to deploy the Church's greatest resource - the people of God. When the body of Christ is successfully mobilised, the possibilities are endless. This mobilisation is one of the greatest needs of the Church today and wherever it is happening the Church is exploding. In Seoul, South Korea, Yonggi Cho has deployed lay ministries so successfully that he has the world's largest church of 800,000 members. Practically everyone in this outstanding church is fully involved in discipleship and ministry programmes.

It is impossible to exaggerate the role of God's people in the ministry. The New Testament teaches that Christ's ministry belongs to all his people and not just to an elite leadership. The Church is the body of Christ. This means that, as a member of Christ's body, you are his agents on the earth and your leaders exist to help you fulfil that role. The classic statement of this is found in Ephesians 4:

> *It was he who gave some to be apostles, some to be prophets, some to be evangelists, and some to be pastors and teachers, [12]to prepare God's people for works of service.*
>
> *(Ephesians 4:11,12)*

God's plan is that every Christian should be actively involved in his work on the earth. It is a call you must not take lightly and cannot avoid if you want to fulfil your personal destiny, because it not just a matter for you. It affects us all. Paul makes it clear that the whole body only grows and develops into maturity as each part does its work.

From him the whole body, joined and held together by every supporting ligament, grows and builds itself up in love, as each part does its work.

(Ephesians 4:16)

Only as everyone takes his place, actively functioning as a member of the body of Christ, will the Church rise up in maturity and strength to take the city for Christ. But how is it to happen? This is a constant challenge to the leaders of Kensington Temple. How do we mobilise so many people into the work of God? We have well over one hundred different nationalities, many congregations meeting centrally and dozens of churches all over the city. Obviously there must be an active and ongoing programme of recruiting and training, but it cannot end there. The goal is to deploy all our members, releasing them into their ministry in the church and society.

This is why we have developed programmes for strategic mobilisation. They are not neat and tidy schemes that work with computer-like precision, but rather great movements or thrusts of activity that explode out of the dynamic life of the central church. Spiritual vitality is released through public preaching, teaching and powerful encounters with the Holy Spirit, and this explosive energy ripples outwards carrying hundreds of people into specific service for Christ.

Recently in Kensington Temple we identified several major areas of spiritual work which the Holy Spirit has called the church to be involved in. These are not programmes in the strict sense, but are ways in which we encourage our people to co-operate with what the Holy Spirit is doing in them. They are proving to be an effective strategy for mobilising the church to reach the city.

This third section of the book outlines this strategy. It will challenge you to find your place in the plan of God. Some of the terms for the areas of ministry and involvement are taken directly from the Scriptures - workmen, ploughmen, watchmen and fishermen. Even though they sound masculine, I have kept them as generic descriptions, applying equally to both men and women.

Workmen

One of the greatest needs of the moment is for Christian workers. We need thousands of men and women totally dedicated to the cause of Christ in our cities, real disciples who have died with Jesus and who live only to fulfil his purpose through their lives. D L Moody, the great American evangelist of last century, was challenged with the words of a preacher who said, "The world has not yet seen what God can do through a man whose life is totally dedicated to him." Moody left the meeting determined to become that man, and what he achieved in his lifetime was truly outstanding.

I respect the achievements of great men and women completely, but I don't think that Christ intends such a level of dedication only for a few isolated individuals. We are all saved for servanthood. The moment we came to Christ we ceased to belong to ourselves.

You acknowledged then, his complete lordship over your spirit, your soul and your body. That means you belong to him entirely. You can hold nothing back; it is all his. This has a twofold implication for your everyday life. There is something to turn away from, and something to embrace. God calls you to reject sin and to pursue righteousness, but it is not enough simply to stop doing the things that preoccupied you before you came to Christ. You must now also take up a new life of righteousness. This is your life of service.

> *Do not offer the parts of your body to sin, as instruments of wickedness, but rather offer yourselves to God, as those who have been brought from death to life; and offer the parts of your body to him as instruments of righteousness.*
>
> *(Romans 6:13)*

The apostle Paul here explains that we are all instruments in this world. It is a fact that cannot be altered, but what can be altered is whose instruments we are. We are either instruments of sin or servants of righteousness. God wants us to present ourselves to him and to dedicate ourselves totally to his service. This is his call upon all his children, and there is no escaping it. Not everyone is called to full time church work, but we are all reserved for full time Christian service, wherever we are in society.

Paul encouraged Timothy to fulfil this call upon his life. He was a pastor, but the principles apply to every call, whether in the arts or the media, in business or commerce, industry or education, whether in the home or in the Church, wherever it is to be worked out. He says,

> *Do your best to present yourself to God as one approved, a workman who does not need to be ashamed and who correctly handles the word of truth.*
>
> *(2 Timothy 2:15)*

As God's workman it was Timothy's first responsibility to present himself to God as one approved. This shows that while God calls us all to be his workmen, he expects a response from us. We cannot take it for granted. There must be a definite decision on our part. It is a transaction that no one can make for us. For me, it was a definite and conscious commitment based on what I knew of Christ the moment I belonged to him. I remember clearly thinking it out in my mind as a very new believer, "If Jesus Christ is worth anything he is worth everything. And if he is my Lord and Saviour then I must give him everything!" Now, I don't claim that I have always lived completely in line with this principle, but I can honestly say that it is what has most consistently governed my choices. I have given my life to him, and that is the end of the matter.

But the call to be his workmen goes much further. Paul instructs Timothy to study, or to make very careful effort to present himself as one approved. What does this mean? Does it mean that God disapproves of some of his children? Or, can it mean that we have to prove ourselves in some way worthy before God? God has no favourites. He does not expect us to win his love or approval, but he does call us to consecrate ourselves and to prepare ourselves for our service for him. Even the Lord Jesus, whose whole life had been given in total consecration to the Father's will, when facing his greatest act of dedication said, "...I sanctify myself..." (John 17:19). That is, he prepared himself totally for the step he was to take in giving his life on the cross.

Paul goes on to spell out to Timothy what that preparation would mean. It was to be a total giving of himself to the knowledge of God through his word. It was God's will for Timothy to be thoroughly equipped for every good work. He was to be a workman so thoroughly prepared that he would never be ashamed. This kind of preparation meant more than simply knowing the theories of sermon construction. It meant a deep knowledge of God's word through the Holy Spirit. It meant that the truth of God's word was to grip Timothy and to hold his conscience captive, producing godly character and rock-like faith.

Many Bible schools and theological training colleges seem to have forgotten that preparation for ministry is first of all about God's approval. It is about getting to know Christ and having one's life in order before him. Some are slow to learn the lesson that academic studies alone are inadequate preparation for the life of Christ in the ministry and, whereas I am not against academic study, I reject totally the notion that a diploma or degree qualifies you for Christian work of any description. Neither am I pleading simply for more practical training to be added to Bible school programmes as anyone can learn the latest clever how-to's. Real Christian ministry is dying to self and allowing the Holy Spirit free access to our private thoughts and feelings, and any public ministry is simply the overflow of these encounters in the secret place.

That is why we have developed our own church-based Bible training programmes. We found from the beginning that this was an effective way to prepare people for ministry. One of our Bible school slogans is "Training at the Cutting Edge." By this we mean that it is all taking place at the cutting edge of active Christian ministry in one of the most exciting churches in the world (of course we are biased!). Something quite unique takes place when people are trained within a live church setting. There is no danger of training becoming an end in itself as the students are inches away from the needs of the city. Those in training cannot opt out of real life and ministry; their stewardship is too precious for us to let it happen.

We have found that training our own leaders has other considerable built in advantages. Most important of all is the developing of leaders who share our heart and ethos as a church. The training philosophy and programme arise out of the vision of the church and so we reproduce exactly the values necessary in ministry to bring it about. Also we are able to train more leaders, more quickly, than traditional Bible colleges. Many colleges are finding it difficult to keep pace even with the requirements of their own denomination, let alone the runaway demands of explosive growth, and this is something the Church must quickly come to terms with as the pace of revival increases. In Britain, we will soon be unable to train all the leaders we need. I have seen the tragedy of inadequate leadership spoiling genuine moves of God in revival many times in my travels in Africa, Asia and South America, and it is already happening in Europe. The failure of communism has left a hunger for Christ in affected nations, resulting in mass conversions. But where are the leaders to take up the work? They are nowhere to be found. We have failed to produce them. The same thing could happen in Britain unless we act now with creative Bible training programmes. I am not suggesting that there is no place for the traditional colleges, but I am saying that there must be much more flexibility in our approach, with colleges and churches working together, sharing their strengths.

Kensington Temple's Bible school, the International Bible Institute of London, provides training at the heart of the life and growth of the central church. With over 350 students at the time of writing we are challenged to provide accessible training programmes with a highly flexible approach to learning methods.

The IBIOL seeks to provide an environment of faith where practical ministry experience goes hand in hand with classroom teaching. Full time one and two year programmes in leadership and ministry are supplemented by short term schools of discipleship, missions, church planting and prophecy. We also have a pioneering course in Creative Ministries. Our goal is to train every believer for front line service, and to encourage the reproduction of training in every local church where we have influence. Only as we remain sensitive to the real needs of church planting and evangelism can we prepare the leaders God wants for a time of unprecedented harvest.

Ploughmen

Every farmer knows that you cannot sow seed into fallow ground. First, it has to be worked. It must be carefully cleared, making sure that all the weeds, rocks and debris are completely removed. Then comes the arduous task of ploughing up the earth. If it is dry and hard it must be softened by gentle rain or by irrigation. All this must happen before anything is planted.

In spiritual terms, our cities are lying fallow. Vast tracts of spiritual wasteland stretch across our cities like long-neglected fields, and land that has never been cultivated. The Ploughman ministry of Kensington Temple takes this seriously and responds to the call of the Spirit, "Plough your fallow ground," given through prophets like Hosea.

> *Sow for yourselves righteousness, reap the fruit of unfailing love, and break up your unplowed ground; for it is time to seek the LORD, until he comes and showers righteousness on you.*
> (Hosea 10:12)

Ploughmen are desperately needed in our cities today to prepare the soil and make it ready for sowing. Before we can successfully sow the seeds of the gospel in an urban area, we must be adequately informed, otherwise we will not be able to pray and plan effectively. Our every effort must be deliberate and targeted if we are going to be successful. Once we know what we are aiming at, we stand a better chance of hitting it.

The power of information

That is why information gathering must be the first step in reaching a city with the gospel. We need to know who is present in an area before we move in with evangelism. We need to know what they are like, what they believe, what their problems are and what their attitude to the gospel is. Once we know about them, we can present the gospel in a way that is relevant to them. We can also find openings into their community and gain acceptance as we genuinely love them where they are, ministering to their felt needs. That is where our Ploughman programme comes in.

It is a strategic attempt to gather information for our citywide vision. We have divided London into zones, each with a structure set up to gather data relevant for prayer, evangelism and church planting. The information gathered from a particular area is processed centrally and made available to those called to work in that area. The organisational structure is a simple one: there are zonal representatives who co-ordinate information gathering in each zone; there are borough representatives to encourage the work in each of London's thirty-three boroughs; and there are hundreds of ploughmen who dig away in their designated locality, finding out all they can to help prepare for the work of outreach in the community. Finally, these workers are themselves covered by intercessors enabling them to get to the spiritual roots of the community as well as gather statistical information.

But just how important is this work? Obviously it is wrong to go insensitively into a community without any knowledge of the people living there, but is it really necessary to take such extreme measures, painstakingly gathering information that may not be needed in the end? Some people think so, preferring to rush straight into soul winning without any research programme. While not totally discounting their point, I want to stress the importance of careful data gathering. If we take the hit-and-miss approach, it will be seen in the long run that it was more miss than hit! We must have a strategy. God expects us to use our brains, provided we are sensitive to his leading while we go about it. We also must be careful to guard against the danger of research for research's sake, and only gather the kind of information that is really helpful for the job at hand.

Why do we need information?

Our teams of ploughmen have shown us again and again the benefits of information gathering. We have found that the following principles, working positively, affect the entire life of the church.

Information gathering is biblical

God told Moses to instruct the children of Israel to gather facts about the promised land as an initial step to obtaining their inheritance.

> *"Send some men to explore the land of Canaan, which I am giving to the Israelites. From each ancestral tribe send one of its leaders."*
>
> *(Numbers 13:2)*

God himself sets the pattern for research; he involves himself in it.

> *For the eyes of the LORD range throughout the earth to strengthen those whose hearts are fully committed to him.*
>
> *(2 Chronicles 16:9)*

> *On that day I swore to them that I would bring them out of Egypt into a land I had searched out for them, a land flowing with milk and honey, the most beautiful of all lands.*
>
> *(Ezekiel 20:6)*

Information gives power

If we are going to help free our cities from the spiritual domination of evil forces, we need to know what is really going on in them. The information we gather will help us get to grips with the problems and alert us to the strategies of the devil in any particular area. It will enable us to pray meaningfully for the release of souls as adequate knowledge of the big picture helps us to intercede with precision. The more we know, the more we can pray, plan and prepare. Generals at war and athletes in competition know that finding out about their opponent's strengths and weaknesses is the first step to victory.

Information brings revelation

When Nehemiah obtained information about his homeland, while in exile, it caused him to mourn and fast for his own sins, for those of his family and for those of his nation. It led him to request a leave of absence from royal service to return to the homeland and rebuild Jerusalem. He gave up the good life in the royal court and faced ridicule and hostility among the people in Israel, but armed with the information he had received, and fired by his own personal call, he caused the discouraged remnant to stand up and cry unanimously,

> *"Let us start rebuilding."*
>
> *(Nehemiah 2:18)*

Information shows our strengths and weaknesses

Information gathering enables us to assess the strength of the enemy and the size of the task ahead. It shows us the level of opposition, the strongholds and the numbers of people we have to reach. It also helps us assess our readiness to take on the task, underlining for us the kind of preparation we need to make. Our researchers have often brought to light the good that is being done by other church groups in an area, showing us how we can assist and complement what is already happening while avoiding unnecessary duplication. Moses counted every male aged twenty and above so that he could determine the strength of his fighting force. Similarly, our information gathering gives us a knowledge of the Church at large and the resources we possess to spread the gospel into targeted areas. Joshua and the rest of the spies came back from their reconnaissance into Canaan with enough information to take the land. Unfortunately, the process exposed an underlying weakness in the nation and they failed to go in because of their unbelief.

They were not ready to do it. In the same way, the proper gathering of information can show us whether we are ready to go ahead with the job or not.

Information gathering helps determine strategy

When an area or people group is ready to receive the gospel, evangelism is easy. It is important to know what the Lord is doing so that we can co-operate with the move of the Holy Spirit. Information on the openness of a group to the gospel can fuel evangelism and give confidence and boldness. It can also direct evangelism. It pays to go to where the harvest is ripe and work with those who are ready to receive. Among those who are not yet ripe for harvest, a different strategy is called for. More prayer is needed. A programme of pre-evangelism, relationship-building and good works will raise people's receptivity to the gospel, and well-researched information will help point the way.

People group thinking

Every evangelistic effort aims to give people an opportunity to know and accept Jesus Christ and to serve him in the fellowship of his Church. The focus therefore is people. God called a people, the Jews, and he sent his servants to other specific peoples. Jonah was sent to the Ninevites, Peter to the Jews and Paul to the Gentiles. We must carry this same people group thinking into our evangelism today.

A people group is a group of men and women with a common affinity. They are unified by language, ethnic origin, geographical location, religion, or economic and social position. New ideas flow readily along lines of natural human relationships. This is obvious from the fact that ideas spread quickly within a close-knit community. Once the gospel successfully penetrates a people group it can spread rapidly through the whole group.

We have adopted a people group approach in our goal to win London for Christ. London is a complex collection of races, cultures and people groups and no one strategy or church can reach every one. We need as many different strategies and churches as there are people groups. Each group will have its own level of response and will require its own presentation of the gospel that corresponds to its needs, attitudes and beliefs. Each group will need its own styles of worship, finding a valid expression within the respective cultures. All this is not simply on ethnic or racial lines, but includes more complex subcultural groups that as yet are not being touched by the ministry of the Church. It will include ravers and unemployed youths on housing estates as well as those who can trace their ethnic origin to Africa, Asia or the Middle East.

Some object to this kind of evangelistic approach, saying that it goes against the gospel principle of unity in Christ. "We are all one in Christ Jesus," they say, "We must drop these ideas about different cultures". Usually people who talk like that are guilty of doing the very thing they think they are avoiding. By ignoring cultural differences, they project a church that says, "If you want to follow Christ you must come to us, dress and talk like us, behave and act like us and worship God exactly the way we do!" The result is that different cultural groups dismiss the Christian Church as irrelevant and continue their spiritual search elsewhere. An active research or data-gathering strategy, such as our Ploughman programme, helps identify these cultural factors and prepares the whole church to receive people from different groups.

So what does the programme involve? First let me point out that the required level of expertise is not high and out of reach. Information gathering is easy, and we help our people by giving them the necessary training. It only takes a few hours of exploring each week, going out into the area you are researching with a number of specific questions in mind.

- What kind of people live here?
- How many are there?
- What are their beliefs and ideas?
- What are their most-keenly felt needs?

Having found out the answers to these questions, we can then ask who is currently seeking to reach a particular group for Christ and how successful they are. We can also look out for some keys to how the community can be penetrated with the gospel. If we are sensitive to the Holy Spirit, he will also show us the spiritual factors that are keeping them from the gospel. All this is invaluable information for those who are going to evangelise that community.

There are many places that our ploughmen have found productive in their quest for information. First, there are the local town halls with the many information booklets they supply and their various departments, such as planning, housing and the social services. Then, there are the libraries which usually keep a great deal of information on the local community including books on local history, local residents and local landmarks. There are also the local police stations which keep reports on major crimes in the area, information on people groups and other helpful statistics. Finally, there are the local action groups formed with the particular needs of an area in mind.

It is all a matter of team work. Ploughmen have the satisfaction of knowing that the information they gather is going to affect the spiritual destiny of people living in the city. Just as intelligence services provide vital information during wartime, often decisively contributing to the outcome of the war, so the ploughmen know that they have a part to play in the victory of Christ in the city.

Watchmen awake!

Having gathered our information together, we then turn it into prayer. We would achieve nothing if it were not for our praying congregation at Kensington Temple. We identify fully with the new worldwide prayer move of the Holy Spirit.

Everywhere I go in the world, I find the Holy Spirit is bringing a new quality in prayer. People are watching and praying, and not just praying the same repetitive prayers again and again. There is a new sense of urgency and we are also learning to be wakeful and alert in the Spirit, listening to God as well as talking to him. It is only then that we see him bring about the changes he has ordained.

It is time that we took up again the chief instruments and weapons that God has given us to bring about his changes on the earth. In a society that is basically founded upon unbelief, we need a praying people who believe that God supernaturally hears and answers prayer. Through prayer we can become the real movers and shapers in our world.

Taking the city by prayer

In April 1991, the Lord directed us at the Kensington Temple Wednesday evening prayer meetings to pray according to Joshua 6, calling us to take London for Jesus.

> *Then the Lord said to Joshua, 'See, I have delivered Jericho into your hands, along with its king and its fighting men'.*
>
> *(Joshua 6:2)*

> *Joshua commanded the people, 'Shout! For the Lord has given you the city!'*
>
> *(Joshua 6:16)*

A new dynamic entered our prayer meetings. Beginning with a renewed commitment from the pastoral staff, the meetings quickly grew from 100 to almost 1,000 in regular attendance. The people gather early and enthusiastically. Expectations run high. The meeting begins with praise and worship, and soon the leaders are heading the troops into battle, the atmosphere charged with a sense of excitement. Strong vibrant intercession comes between sessions of victory shouts and spontaneous clapping as the sense of triumph bursts out upon the praying people, everyone joining in with the same spirit of determination and spiritual aggression as the army rises up to take the kingdom by force.

We make every effort to include all the various modes of biblical prayer. There are sessions of quiet prayer in small groups, contemplative prayer, corporate tongues and carefully placed assaults on the enemy. However, the dominant themes are praise and warfare. They are times of powerful confrontation with the forces of darkness as the Lord establishes his kingdom through his praying people on earth.

> *Your kingdom come, your will be done on earth as it is in heaven.*
>
> *(Matthew 6:10)*

The prayer meetings do not systematically cover every area of church life and ministry. Rather they are led with sensitivity to the Spirit's mind and will, with a strong emphasis on prophetic direction. The staff and leaders meet earlier in the day to listen to what the Spirit is saying and revelation frequently flows during the meeting, each insight carefully recorded for further confirmation and action, as appropriate. All this goes hand in hand with careful planning and research involving members of the staff and congregation alike. The meetings themselves are a spearhead. Like a gigantic ploughshare, the Wednesday evening prayer meeting breaks up the ground and leads the way for other smaller prayer meetings in homes and numerous fellowship groups throughout the week. The topics are wide ranging, reflecting the church's vision for world evangelism as well as national influence in social, moral and political matters.

Despite all this, I was still burdened about the need for intercession, and one Sunday evening I ministered on the subject of intercessors acting as watchmen for the city, from Isaiah 62:6,7.

> *I have posted watchmen on your walls, O Jerusalem; they will never be silent day or night. You who call on the LORD, give yourselves no rest, and give him no rest till he establishes Jerusalem and makes her the praise of the earth.*
>
> *(Isaiah 62:6,7)*

Suddenly, in the middle of the message, I felt compelled by the Holy Spirit to call out, "Watchmen awake!" Many people stood in response to the challenge and the Lord released a powerful anointing on them. That was the beginning of the Kensington Temple Watchman programme.

The watchmen of the city

In ancient times cities were built as places of refuge and protection. They were ruled by kings and guarded by soldiers garrisoned in the citadels. People would come under the safety and security of their city and were enabled to live together in peace. As an essential part of defence, high walls of protection were built around the entire city and once the gates were closed, the city would be secure from outside attackers. Some could survive for many years under siege as long as there was essential provision of food and water within.

High watchtowers were often built into the city walls and from these vantage points the watchmen would be on duty day and night. They could see visitors or messengers far off and warn of impending attacks from enemies. Their responsibility was to be vigilant and faithfully report what they saw to the city officials.

In the same way today, the Lord has stationed his modern day watchmen on the walls of the city. In seeking to understand this we must appreciate that it is the Lord who positions his watchmen. He said of Jerusalem, "I have posted watchmen on your walls." This is absolutely crucial. No pastor or prayer rota can do it. When watchmen hear the call of the Spirit there is an urgency, a sense of strategic importance. Many have already heard and answered the call and they pray out the revelation God has given them in the secret place, under a powerful anointing. It is true that every Christian is called to a lifestyle of prayer, but the watchman's burden is greater than that.

The watchman call also reveals that there is a strategic significance to night time praying "...they will never be silent day or night". Jesus had his darkest hour at night. His disappointment was clearly evident when he asked his disciples to watch and pray with him, but they fell asleep.

> *Could you men not keep watch with me for one hour?*
> *(Matthew 26:40)*

It is important for watchmen to be vigilant even during the night time. There was particular pressure and strain on the night watchmen, as enemies would frequently attack in the small hours. The night is a cloak for evil when many literal works of darkness take place. It is our duty to be alert and to pray against these things, and there is a much greater place for all night prayer vigils than we have ever understood.

> *My soul waits for the Lord more than watchmen wait for the morning, more than watchmen wait for the morning.*
>
> (Psalm 130:6)

The Watchman ministry

In order to watch and pray effectively you need to understand all the functions of spiritual watchmen that are revealed in the Scriptures. They are all relevant to you in your church, city, and nation today.

Revelation

If we believe there is something wrong with what is happening around us, we should petition Almighty God. As Christians, we should be active in expressing our opinions by writing, protesting and petitioning state leaders, but we should always remember that God is on the throne. If we believe this, we will spend more time petitioning the Almighty. But in order to pray accurately we need to receive revelation. When we pray according to revelation, we know our prayers will be on target and that we will see God answer.

Habakkuk was a prophet called to minister to the people of God at a crucial time in the history of the nation of Judah, when the growing Babylonian empire threatened to engulf Judah. He petitioned God with several complaints, as he could not understand how God could allow such a wicked nation to attack his people.

> *"I will stand at my watch and station myself on the ramparts, I will look to see what he will say to me, and what answer I am to give to this complaint."*
>
> (Habakkuk 2:1)

Habakkuk got his reply. The Lord had no intention of ignoring the sins of Babylon but he was actually raising up an army against his disobedient people to bring judgement on them. Like Habakkuk, watchmen today are to be alert to what God is doing. Beyond the political editorials in the newspapers, we should be looking to the Lord, hearing from him, and discerning his purposes in the world. God wants to raise up a church that will be able to speak into the national and international arena, having first heard from him.

Intercession

Watchmen are called to a lifestyle of intercession based on what they have seen and heard by revelation. Intercession must flow out of revelation. Too many people pray with insufficient knowledge, seeking to pray their own will into being, but these are not prayers God answers. He answers prayers prayed in accordance with his will. In Gethsemane, Jesus aligned himself, despite his own personal feelings, with the purpose of God,

> *"Not my will, but yours be done."*
>
> *(Luke 22:42)*

For example, what if it were God's will to bring ever deepening recession into Britain so that we no longer put our faith in money? How would he lead us to pray? It would not be right to ask God to set Britain free from the recession. We would have to cry out to the Lord for him to deepen the recession and bring the nation literally to its knees! So often we pray according to our comfort, putting our needs and considerations first, but God's purposes go far higher than that. God is concerned about us and our needs, and wants to minister to them, but above all, his great agenda is to see his name honoured and his kingdom come. This goes right against the grain of what many of us expect from a life of prayer.

Isaiah 62 brings out the intercessory nature of the watchman call. God shows the prophet that not only is he called to bring the word of the Lord to the people of God, but he is also called to intercede. All the great prophets were great prayers. You have to be an intercessor to bring the word of God into any situation because it's not a comfortable thing to do. This is the spirit of the watchman that came upon Isaiah.

> *For Zion's sake I will not keep silent, for Jerusalem's sake I will not remain quiet, till her righteousness shines out like the dawn, her salvation like a blazing torch.*
>
> *(Isaiah 62:1)*

God says,

> *"I have posted watchmen on your walls, O Jerusalem; they will never be silent day or night. You who call on the Lord, give yourselves no rest, and give him no rest till he establishes Jerusalem and makes her the praise of the earth."*
>
> *(Isaiah 62:6,7)*

This is a classic picture of intercession. The watchmen stand upon the high walls of intercession and, from that vantage point, watch and pray. The first person that should hear about our concerns is God. We bring back to him in prayer and intercession all the things he has revealed to us concerning his will on the earth.

Praise

Another key role in the work of watchmen is praise. We rejoice as watchmen, because we can see what God is doing.

> *Listen! Your watchmen lift up their voices; together they shout for joy. When the Lord returns to Zion, they will see it with their own eyes.*
>
> *(Isaiah 52:8)*

Here the prophet speaks of the watchmen leading the way in the praises of God. Watchmen didn't have to be gifted singers or musicians. They weren't necessarily worship leaders, but they were the first to see the good news. When God begins to move, the watchmen are the first to know about it. We are not just waiting for revival to come to London. In one sense revival has already begun. The watchmen have already seen it in the heavenlies. There are certain clear indications that show what is happening in the spiritual realm over Britain as we see signs of renewal in many places. The Holy Spirit is reversing years of spiritual decline.

One of our ministers was travelling by train on the continent when he noticed a large group of British people. He began to talk to them and discovered that they were all witches, travelling to a special witchcraft convention. The reason they went abroad to practise their witchcraft elsewhere was that they had discovered the level they were seeking to operate in now no longer works in Britain!

This new spiritual atmosphere is because Christians have been praying and praising God with praise marches, prayer walks, whole nights of prayer, intercession and fasting. The result is an opening in the heavenly realms over Britain. This is one of the indications we have seen that a change is taking place.

The gospel is spreading like wildfire among many people groups in Britain, as people simply tell their friends and families about Jesus at a grass roots level. I believe that this is the beginning of a significant move of God, and I confidently expect that if we remain faithful it will grow into revival. Many people focus on the problems all around them and ask, "Where is the revival?" If we only view things from an earthly perspective, there is much to discourage us. But come and stand with me on the ramparts and have a look. You will see the revival! Revival begins in the heavenlies. Nothing of God comes down to the earth unless it is first achieved in heaven.

The watchmen are seeing all these things even before others are aware of them, and this is right in line with their calling.

> *Burst into songs of joy together, you ruins of Jerusalem, for the Lord has comforted his people, he has redeemed Jerusalem."*
>
> *(Isaiah 52:9)*

These words were spoken before the need was even perceived by the people of Judah. Over 100 years before Israel's exile, the Holy Spirit showed Isaiah that the Jews would return to their homeland. And when the time drew near for the prophecy to be fulfilled the exiles could accept it as an accomplished fact. The prophet was saying, "It has happened, even though you don't yet see it." The evidence was that the watchmen were rejoicing. In the same way today, prophetic watchmen are hearing from God and praising him for what they know he is about to do.

Proclamation

> *"Son of man, I have made you a watchman for the house of Israel; so hear the word I speak and give them warning from me. [18]When I say to a wicked man, 'You will surely die,' and you do not warn him or speak out to dissuade him from his evil ways in order to save his life, that wicked man will die for his sin, and I will hold you accountable for his blood. [19]But if you do warn the wicked man and he does not turn from his wickedness or from his evil ways, he will die for his sin; but you will have saved yourself."*
>
> *(Ezekiel 3:17-19)*

All the prophets were called to be watchmen. Like Ezekiel, they were to hear from God and tell the people what they heard. Watchmen are called to proclaim from their vantage point of prophetic revelation. Proclamation has two parts: telling God's people the wonderful things we see him doing in the heavenlies, and bringing warning from God concerning the spiritual state of the Church and the nation.

We have a great responsibility to obey God and not keep silent about what he tells us. When he tells us, as his watchmen, to bring warning, we dare not disobey. We must stand up and speak the word of the Lord to our society with authority, clarity and conviction.

Protection

Prayer protection is vital for leaders as we move forward in faith to take our cities for God. Without it we dare not put one foot in front of the other. It is highly dangerous for leaders to underestimate the power of the enemy or foolishly to go ahead without adequate prayer cover.

In the 1980's many ministries ended in tragedy. Terminal illness, marital and financial ruin, and fatal accidents all took their toll on precious ministries God had given to the nations. The reason, above all, was that there was insufficient prayer cover. The Church failed to pray at all or failed to pray effectively. Ignorance of the true situation in the heavenlies and ignorance of the effective counter measures we have through our authority in Christ lay behind much of our failure. This was sadly coupled with a general indifference and prayerlessness. The results were catastrophic and we cannot let it happen again. In the 1990's the Lord wants to raise up even more powerful and effective ministries. We must not fail them; he holds us responsible as his watchmen.

We will never know the pressures that are upon significant men and women of God today. When someone takes a strong stand for the Lord, he becomes a special target of the enemy. Agents of Satan often infiltrate our church services with malevolent aims against the leadership. This is especially true of leaders effective for God. The New Testament teaches that there is an invisible, unseen world at the head of which is Satan, the god of this age. Thank God that another invisible power is at work - the mighty power of God's kingdom manifested to destroy Satan and his evil works!

We need people who will minister, not just with words, but with mighty demonstrations of the Holy Spirit's power. We need more men like Wesley, who, according to some, averted Great Britain from a revolution such as the one in France, and men like Spurgeon of the last century who shook London with the word of God. They were valiant warriors of the faith, fighting under the anointing of the Holy Spirit.

The Lord is raising up people like that today. We need to cover them and protect them. They need protection and help more than we can ever know. If Jesus the Lord of glory asked his disciples to pray and watch with him for one hour, how much more do today's spiritual leaders need it. People in leadership are not superhuman. They are often weak individuals set apart only by the call of God on their lives. If you see any Christian in the public eye, or anybody being powerfully used of God in any way at all, cover them in prayer. Watch and stand guard over them, giving them all the spiritual protection you can.

Psalm 127:1 shows us one of the key functions of the watchmen in Old Testament times. They were the city's first line of defence. When an army came to attack, the watchmen standing guard on the city walls would warn those inside so they could prepare to defend themselves.

> *Unless the Lord watches over the city, the watchmen stand guard in vain.*
>
> *(Psalm 127:1)*

Here the psalmist is emphasising that the Lord is the real Watchman, but he also shows that the role of earthly watchmen is to protect the city. We are called to do this in the Spirit, building up the walls of prayer around the entire city.

Warfare

Monstrous spiritual forces hold the cities and nations of the world in terror and bondage. Like mighty Goliaths they have gone unchallenged for centuries, but their time is up! Jesus will yet prove himself victorious through his Church. However, we are not ignorant of the devil's schemes and tactics. We do not fight against flesh and blood, but against principalities and powers. Therefore our weapons are spiritual and not fleshly. Fully clothed with the whole armour of God, we pray in the Spirit on all occasions and with all kinds of prayers.

God revealed to the Old Testament prophets that he had raised the Babylonians up as an instrument to bring judgement upon Judah, but when the time came, they overstepped the mark. They tried to annihilate God's people totally, and instead of bringing judgement they brought almost total destruction. So God determined to judge Babylon. Jeremiah prophesied the fall of Babylon, and in so doing he gave us a glimpse of the role of watchmen in spiritual warfare.

> *Lift up a banner against the walls of Babylon! Reinforce the guard. Station the watchmen, prepare an ambush. The LORD will carry out his purpose, his decree against the people of Babylon.*
>
> *(Jeremiah 51:12)*

We must never forget that our true enemies are spiritual. The men who are holding captive many in our nation through pornography, satanism and drug dealing, as wicked as they are, need the love of Jesus. We are fighting against spiritual forces that are operating through people who have given themselves over to Satan. The Holy Spirit is raising up a spiritually militant Church that will know how to deal with this flood tide of iniquity. Our weapons are spiritual, and prayer is our protective covering as we move forward.

In a certain African nation where Christianity is repressed by some state authorities due to the influence of a dominant anti-Christian religion, one pastor went to the chief authority to ask permission to build a church. Up to that point, permission had been withheld, although the constitution of that nation provides for freedom of religion. This pastor didn't take a petition. He didn't form a protest. He and his church simply prayed. Then he went to the man in authority and said, "Are you going to give me this church, or are you not? But before you reply, know that the way you answer me determines how I shall deal with you in the Spirit." He got the permission!

These are important, strategic days, and we need to realise the power God has given us through prayer and take it seriously. He has chosen to work through militant and powerful prayer. As watchmen we must step up our efforts of spiritual warfare. In wartime, the numbers of watchmen are doubled and redoubled. As there is an intensive spiritual war going on in the heavenlies over the nations of the world at this very moment it is essential that we take up our positions as watchmen. We must defend the Church against the onslaught and to go on the offensive against Satan's positions.

Although he is very powerful, we know that Satan is already defeated. God has equipped us and he is training our hands for battle, to be on the attack and inflict great damage to the enemy. God has ordained praise to silence the foe and the avenger, and it is with the high praises of God in our mouths, with the two edged sword of God's word in our hands, that we move forward to execute God's written judgement on our enemy.

Preparation

We can look forward to a significant time of outpouring and expansion. The Lord wants to work among us in power and to bring in a fresh move of his Spirit that will eclipse anything we have seen so far. This will mean an unprecedented mobilisation of men and women into ministries in their own cities and further afield. The result of what God is doing will be even greater growth and expansion than we have yet seen. There are countless thousands of people throughout the world who will hear and believe the Lord's message. They will come and see the glory of God among us. However, all this is not inevitable. It must be prayed into place as God acts in response to his people's prayers. Nothing less than a powerful army of prayerful people interceding day and night throughout this decade will fulfil God's mandate.

> *The watchman opens the gate for him, and the sheep listen to his voice. He calls his own sheep by name and leads them out.*
> *(John 10:3)*

The familiar story of the Good Shepherd reveals an exciting truth about the watchman ministry that many miss. In the cities the watchmen would let the gatekeeper know there was somebody coming, so they could see who it was and open the gates. The watchmen prepared the way for those who wanted to enter the city. But in the shepherdly context, we have the picture of a watchman whose station of watch was a sheep pen. During the day the shepherds would take their separate flocks out to pasture, but at night they would all be mingled together in the watchman's sheep pen. The shepherds would entrust their sheep to the watchman, who would watch and protect them overnight. In the morning when the shepherds came, the watchman would open the gate, and each shepherd would call his sheep and lead them out to fresh pasture.

This is an excellent analogy for the role of the watchmen who open the gate for the coming of Jesus. Jesus Christ stands outside the gates of your city right now and the key to opening the door and letting him in is in the hands of the watchmen who open the gate for Jesus to come in. It is vital for the watchmen to fulfil the mandate to watch and to pray. When the Lord visits a city, the first thing he will do is call out his people and set them free. His sheep will hear his voice and they will follow him, and there will be a mass turning to the Lord Jesus Christ.

The watchman commitment

At Kensington Temple we ask our watchmen to make a two-fold commitment. First, they must cultivate a lifestyle of prayer. Without making it a hard and fast rule, most people consider that the minimum requirement for this ministry is to spend an hour each day in effective prayer. This needs to be cultivated, as to maintain this level of consistency requires discipline over one's entire activities. We simply set this out as a desirable goal, but each person must find his own level in the Lord, remembering that it is the quality of his prayer life that counts, not simply the length of time he actually spends praying.

The second commitment is to pray for one hour at a set time each week using prayer topics relating to specific needs in the life and ministry of the church. In particular, the call centres on three main areas, praying for the family, the church and the city or nation.

We have at least one thousand watchmen regularly in place in Kensington Temple. Without their ministry we have inadequate prayer cover. God wants you also to hear the voice of Jesus as he calls you to take your position seriously and be faithful as you watch and pray, not in your own strength, but as you are empowered by the Holy Spirit. Together, we have authority to tread down every work of Satan, and we can do all things through Christ who strengthens us. We fight with the word of the Lord which never returns to him void, but accomplishes what he desires and achieves the purpose for which he sent it. So, watchmen, hear the word of the Lord, "Rise up! Stand at your post! Watch and pray!"

As soon as the watchmen were in place, the Lord showed us the next step.

Fishermen

Jesus launched his mission to reach the world with the love of God and altered the entire course of history with the words he spoke to his disciples,

> *"Come, follow me, and I will make you fishers of men."*
>
> *(Mark 1:17)*

Thereafter, Jesus lived with the men he called, ate with them and demonstrated the kingdom of God among them daily. After three years he left them fully trained, equipped and empowered by the Holy Spirit to carry on his work. And so the great work of the Church began. Mark records,

> *Then the disciples went out and preached everywhere, and the Lord worked with them and confirmed his word by the signs that accompanied it.*
>
> *(Mark 16:20)*

Called to tell

God's plan has not changed; his methods are the same. Jesus Christ is still exalted at the Father's right hand. He is still directing his disciples on earth, and the call still rings out,

> *"Go into all the world and preach the good news to all creation."*
>
> *(Mark 16:15)*

The responsibility to preach the gospel continues to rest with the disciples of Christ. It is not simply the job of a few evangelists or apostolic figures, but is the task of the whole Church.

Whenever ordinary believers in Jesus have understood this fundamental principle, the church has exploded. There is no substitute for the simple, direct testimony of believers sharing their faith. Even great evangelists like Billy Graham and Reinhard Bonnke cannot be effective in their ministry without us. They are the salesmen, and we are the satisfied customers publicising by word of mouth what Jesus Christ has done for us. Over 90% of people come to Christ through the personal witness of a friend or relative. Nearly everyone who responds to the gospel during public evangelistic campaigns has been personally invited or brought through the witness of another Christian. We are all called to be fishers of men, through the day-to-day living out of our faith and through speaking to others about Jesus. That is the only way that the millions without the gospel will receive it.

At the present time, over one third of the world's population claims a Christian allegiance. This is a staggering statistic, and it is a great testimony to Christ's love and power at work in the world today. But there is another picture. One in four people worldwide have never heard the gospel because we have not yet told them. We have not gone to where they are and shared the good news in a way that they can understand and accept. World evangelism is the uppermost priority of the Church. We cannot deny this and remain true to Christ. That is why we emphasise evangelism so much in Kensington Temple. We are all called to witness, whether to our next door neighbour or to people on the other side of the world.

Ashamed of Jesus?

If all of this is true, why are we so slow to do it? Why is it that very few Christians lead an evangelistic lifestyle? There are many reasons, but the main one is quite simply fear. Fear binds and controls us, ensuring that we are not vocal about our beliefs. After all, no one likes being ridiculed, and often that is how the world responds to Christians who are open about their faith. Perhaps we are afraid we will not be able to answer their questions. We might not be very sure about our faith or feel skilled in presenting the gospel, so we feel a sense of personal inadequacy. What can be done about it?

First of all, we must have confidence - not in ourselves, but in the Lord. He has promised to be with us. Alongside his command to go and make disciples of all nations, Jesus said:

> *"And surely I am with you always, to the very end of the age."*
> *(Matthew 28:20)*

His presence with us is not passive. He works with us as we speak for him. He brings the conviction of the Holy Spirit, adding weight to what we say and confirming his word with signs following. These may be healings, miracles and other gifts of the Holy Spirit. But there can also be the simple testimony of the Holy Spirit, coming through external circumstances or an inner witness that says the gospel is true. We must remember that people's initial reactions may not always betray what is really going on in their hearts. So we can depend on the Lord to give us a boldness in the Holy Spirit which will overcome any timidity on our part and cause us to take the opportunities to witness that come to us daily. Personally, I have to make a conscious decision to witness every time, but the Lord has never failed me yet.

Our fishermen are finding that God is working with them in remarkable ways with miraculous healings and dramatic conversions taking place on the streets. Stefan, a member of one of our outreach teams, met a man in the Portobello market who was limping. "Do you believe Jesus can heal you?" Stefan asked him. He was fairly non-committal, but the young evangelist boldly replied, "If Jesus does heal you right now, then believe in him!" All the pain went and the man was healed instantly. More and more healings are happening in public places as we take the gospel onto the streets.

Perhaps one of the most dramatic conversions came during the dress rehearsal for our Christmas play one year. Ravi, a recently converted Christian was playing the part of Gabriel. Dressed in an angel costume, complete with long hair, wings and a three foot sword, he went outside the church during a break. As a man approached him he descended the steps to the pavement. Pointing his sword at the man he declared, "Jesus loves you." After a few moments the man realised that Ravi was a real person and not a supernatural being - but the encounter was indeed supernatural. The man was on his way to commit suicide. He had made one last desperate cry to a God he didn't know and didn't think would answer him in any tangible way. He gave his life to Christ.

Love constrains

There is something else we can do to remove the barriers to witness. I find that personal witness flows out of love. Think about it for a moment. When you really care for people, you want the very best for them. That means you want them to have Jesus! Our love for people will give us courage to overcome fear and speak out for Christ. And people are ready to listen. Over the last twenty years, there has been a complete change in the attitudes of ordinary people in Britain. They now want to hear about Christ. There are more conversions taking place today than there have been in many years. The spiritual appetite of the nation is increasing. Years of decadent living dominated by materialism and immorality have produced emptiness and dissatisfaction in thousands of people. Britain is ripe for evangelism. London is ready for the gospel. For the love of Jesus we must give it to them.

Even in areas hostile to the gospel, God is revealing his love. One Saturday night, the pastor of our Earl's Court satellite church was challenged by Bill, a homosexual, to "come into a gay bar to prove she didn't hate gay people." Taking one of her congregation with her, Linda walked bravely into the club, where, "everything you can imagine" was going on. They shared the gospel with Bill, who asked them to pray for him. Somewhat bemused, but nevertheless willing, Linda prayed for Bill as he knelt down in the middle of the dance floor in full view of all the men in the club. The power and love of God know no boundaries.

The Fisherman programme

Following the success of Kensington Temple's Watchman programme that mobilised over 1,000 people into ongoing intercession, the Fisherman initiative was conceived to help release the church into active evangelism. The fisherman pledges to cultivate a lifestyle of evangelism, committing time to at least one regular evangelistic activity and endeavouring to make the most of every opportunity to witness for Christ.

Regular street outreaches take place in London's West End and Portobello Road, one of London's most famous street markets. Teams of workers from Kensington Temple can frequently be found witnessing through music, drama, preaching and praying for the sick. We also mobilise teams into areas where our ploughmen (researchers) have been working and where new churches are being planted. However, not all evangelism is so public. We encourage the fishermen to undertake ongoing training in lifestyle evangelism, enabling people who are naturally part of their everyday lives to hear the gospel. The way we live can be a powerful witness.

Most people are led to Christ by someone who has been a believer for less than eighteen months. This is because after that time most new Christians lose meaningful contact with non-Christians. Our own lifestyle can change so radically that we have to work hard to maintain any friendship links with people who do not yet know Jesus. We crowd our lives so full of meetings and Christian based activities that we often don't have time for our unbelieving friends. The Fisherman programme aims to change that by encouraging people to make and maintain contact with people through such things as sport or music. We suggest regular dinner parties and social evenings where Christians and non-Christians can meet. On these occasions the conversation soon moves on to spiritual matters, and as relationships deepen trust develops and people give their lives to Christ. One approach is for a group of two or three fishermen to meet regularly to pray for their non-Christian friends and relatives. During these times they also plan and prepare ways to witness, perhaps meeting their friends on a regular basis for a meal or a game of squash. It is surprising how natural sharing their faith becomes in situations like these.

Partnership of ministries

The fishermen are able to meet regularly for conferences, where there is a healthy pooling of resources and exchange of ideas. With the many different approaches and styles of evangelism we have we can all learn from each other. There is a network of ministries, with some people specialising in certain areas such as youth work, street work and reaching addicts and prostitutes with the gospel. The watchmen and the fishermen work together ensuring that there is strong prayer support for the evangelism that we do. The pattern is for the ploughmen to go into an area first, to gather helpful information. This is then fed to the intercessors who pray, and to the evangelism co-ordinators who begin to devise suitable evangelistic strategies. And when the time for evangelism comes the fishermen are given strong prayer cover, with the intercessors often meeting in the area to "cleanse" the spiritual atmosphere. Many are coming to Christ as a result, ready for the next phase in the strategy.

Calling all church planters!

Church planting is now an established part of Church life in Britain. Every major denomination or church group currently has a church planting programme. A few years ago there was hardly one course on church planting available, but now the subject is being covered in dozens of seminars, training programmes and Bible colleges across the nation. Changing attitudes and increasing awareness of the need to plant churches have come through the church growth movement. Church growth experts say that church groups involved in church planting are growing in overall membership, while those with no church planting programme are declining. Without exception, every denomination which is growing is also involved in church planting.

We need thousands of new churches so that everyone in Britain will be within easy reach of a church that preaches and lives the gospel in a relevant way. We need a church for every community. This is now the considered opinion of every major church group in the country. At the Challenge 2,000 conference in Birmingham early in 1992, a goal was set by all the major British church groups to double the church attendance in Britain by the end of the century. In church planting terms, this means another 20,000 churches, each with at least 150 attenders, for the whole of Britain, with London needing 7,000 new churches.

Kensington Temple's vision is totally in line with this thinking. We have been planting churches from the mid 1980's, sensing the need to penetrate London with live gospel communities, preaching and being good news across the city. In 1985, I founded the first official Kensington Temple satellite church, in Barnet, North London. The group began to meet as a church in the large lounge of one of the members. The fellowship had been in existence for around ten years, meeting first as a nurses' Christian fellowship in the local hospital. We began with a regular Sunday evening service and soon a thriving church was in evidence. With that was born Kensington Temple's vision to see London saturated with a network of churches reaching out into every community in the city. We now have a goal to see 2,000 of these established.

This goal is realisable. We already have the capacity to plant one new church each week. But the greatest need is for willing workers to fulfil this vision. Church planting is tough. It is much easier to sit comfortably in a church that is already well established as it is far less demanding. Church planting requires a pioneer spirit and a very determined bunch of people who refuse to get discouraged. The vision of taking London for Christ must be strong enough to sustain the growth pains throughout the period of the church's infancy, its adolescence and into its maturity.

Church planting can also be a lot of fun. I remember with hilarity my early attempts at preaching and leading meetings, almost twenty years ago. Not known for my singing ability, I had the most disastrous effect upon many a pioneer congregation struggling to master the mystery of my song-leading. It was like playing a game of who can find the right key, or during more desperate moments, any key will do! In the earliest days of my preaching career, I remember cornering two elderly ladies following afternoon tea one Sunday and insisting they listen to me preach my first sermon. It was entitled, "God Resisteth the Proud," and it lasted for over 90 minutes. Their subsequent comments were quite humbling! Another time I was attempting to climb the heights of homiletical delivery on the subject of the

Incarnation, which I described as, "The Supreme Act of Divine Condensation!" Fortunately, they didn't stone me as a false prophet or burn me as a heretic. In fact, they didn't even notice my verbal slip. They were either fast asleep or wishing the preacher was invisible as well as incomprehensible!

Reports from many pioneers suggest that the situation has not changed much. Beginners are still making their mistakes, but at least they are having a go. Over the years we have learned not to despise the day of small things. We have also picked up a little knowledge along the way as to how to go about planting urban churches. One thing is certain: there is no one right way to do it. We do not set an inflexible model of church planting but encourage people to be sensitive to the Holy Spirit, each other and those they are trying to reach. We suggest people spend adequate time praying and preparing for the church plant. We insist on training, although most of it can be done in ministry. We offer little if anything by way of financial assistance, preferring rather to create an environment of faith so that anyone who is called to plant a church can go out and do it.

Soke Mun, a dentist working in the Wembley area was leading many people to Christ through her work (in such a vulnerable position, I feel sure people are more open hearted as well as open mouthed!) With her friend Vanessa, she began to realise that there needed to be a fellowship for these new converts to be cared for and discipled. They prayed for many months together before they received the word from God, "Go for it - the time is right." Starting with ten committed members they prayed and fasted and a strategy was formed to begin evangelising the area - especially the housing estates. The big breakthrough came when a patient in Soke Mun's surgery suggested they could meet in a room in a pub, aptly named "The Lord's Bar." The church was born.

We have seen churches grow out of small fellowship groups while others begin with one or two key leaders with a strong call to a certain area of London. In this way we have started many churches within London's ethnic groups.

In 1988, a young Cantonese Christian felt the increasing burden to start a Pentecostal church for older Cantonese speaking people, and for English speaking young Cantonese who felt like outsiders in an English church. Joshua believed it was God's time to change this situation and launched a group of about twenty people as a Chinese speaking church, determined to make its mark on the Chinese community in Soho. From the start, the church was highly structured with four team leaders, each with their own specific ministry. Now, just five years later, the church has experienced substantial growth with office premises, a full time secretary, and two services on a Sunday: one in Cantonese, one in English.

We have sizeable churches for Arabs, Eritreans, Filipinos, Portuguese and many other people groups. We have also launched churches by sending out large numbers of our membership, both our best leaders and at times the less experienced, into areas of London where there was no strong church.

Although there are no hard and fast rules in this we have found a few sound principles. We give the following advice to those who are called to plant churches with us:

Make sure you believe in the vision for church planting.
It is amazing how once you have this vision you can hang on, even through the difficult times.

Make sure you spend adequate time in preparation.
Just as a human life begins with a period of gestation in the womb, so a church must be conceived and begin to be formed

before it is born. Without this preparation and prayerful planning there will be no church. A realistic look at your gifts and skills at this stage will help with the process of building the church planting team. We encourage strong team work in order to share the load. Training is also essential and we insist on it in every case, but have a flexible training programme that is suitable for every level of experience and development.

Make sure you are committed to the whole satellite church structure.
As mentioned in Part Two of this book, our goal is for a city church, and not simply to plant isolated churches doing their own thing separate from the central thrust of the vision. We have an overall leader of our church planting programme as well as leaders over London zones, and these work together to help oversee our satellite churches.

The church planting programme is the final thrust in the strategy for mobilising the church to reach London for Christ. The ploughmen till the soil, turning up data that can be taken by the watchmen who intercede accordingly, and used by the fishermen who move in and evangelise. Finally, the church planters arrive and disciple the believers into a fully fledged Christian church that in turn reaches out into the community.

All these things are achieved by small groups of people working in teams. The overall vision is carried by the cell life of the church.

Power cell discipleship

Large but personal - in Kensington but touching Lambeth, Brent, Essex and Middlesex - dynamic, fast moving but caring. How is this possible? How is it possible to place a high value on discipleship and still be such a large church? We value not only celebration, prayer and social action, but also radical, personal discipleship. How can care, accountability and friendship be developed when the congregation numbers in the thousands? The answer is through a dynamic, high profile programme of small groups.

There are two prominent New Testament words that describe this. They are both relationship words. *Koinonia*, translated fellowship, means partnership or participation. We are in fellowship with each other because we are in common ownership of Christ. We are in communion with him and with each other. *Ekklesia*, translated church, means a gathering of those who have come out of the world and have joined up with Jesus.

From these two words, we can see that we do not merely have times of fellowship; we are in a fellowship relationship with each other all the time. Neither do we simply go to church; we are the Church. Both these relationships exist twenty four hours a day. If we are to be true to this calling and give full expression to who we are as God's people, we will not limit all activities of fellowship or church to the meetings. For many people, church ends with the benediction and fellowship ends in the car park or at the bus stop! We need to go much further than that. The early Church met daily, giving full expression to every aspect of their lives together in *koinonia* and *ekklesia*. Church services and meetings are designed to refresh us and equip us to go out and be the church for the rest of the week. Mere Sunday Christians know nothing of this.

The Power Cell programme gives people an opportunity to function as who they really are in the body of Christ. It is a vital part of the ministry to the whole city. It is the most basic and readily accessible unit of church involvement and releases our people to be the church right where they are - in their homes, at their places of work or wherever there is an opportunity to meet in small groups. It is here that people meet to care for each other, to interact around the Bible, to see personal breakthroughs in prayer, to reach friends and encourage each other's walk with Jesus. It is not possible to produce matured disciples simply through large meetings, so people are encouraged to be involved in small groups as well as on a celebration level.

In the 1980's the Kensington Temple focus was upon special interest groups. People met together on the basis of special interest and the groups were made up of ethnic and professional fellowships. We found that people most effectively ministered to other people who were like them. So groups mushroomed around London - groups of architects, lawyers, professional footballers, people from South-East Asia, Africa, the Caribbean and many other parts of the world. They met together with the purpose of winning colleagues and people from their part of the world. The effects were startling - conversions, communities penetrated and churches started.

We also had what we called Care Groups, which were the more general house groups of the church. We looked upon these small groups as microcosmic churches - little units of *ekklesia*, and it was here that the basic level of pastoral care happened. Eight or ten people would meet for Bible study and prayer, and would receive pastoral care. The groups also became the centre of the social life of the church as well as a means of evangelising local areas. So through this ministry specific people groups were being reached, local areas were evangelised and the congregation was receiving pastoral care.

In the 1990's we developed the small group ministry still further with our Power Cell programme which brings people together with a common purpose or activity. The purpose might be intercession, evangelism or social action, but whatever the activity, the group is united behind it. The desire is to produce a body of believers who are truly active for Christ. The groups were launched by a powerful sermon entitled "Doers of the Word", preached one Sunday to all six congregations and disseminated throughout the whole church by cassette. This sermon focussed upon the need for the body, not only to hear the words of Jesus but also to be active participants. The power cells were shown to be one of the primary ways to express this dynamic life and consequently had a strong and dynamic foundation on which to build.

All this is helping the commitment of the church to the small group concept. Imagine groups all over a city interceding for its welfare, groups sharing the gospel with friends, groups helping the poor, the elderly and the needy. Imagine your city populated by small cells of life pulsating with the power and presence of Jesus! At the same time these "doers of the word" are getting to know each other, praying for each other and caring for each other.

Our Power Cell programme incorporates four different type of cell:

Intercession groups are involved in a two way prayer exchange. They receive strategic prayer items from the main church and also report back to the leadership prayer information that God gives them. In this way the intercession groups are a key part of the prayer ministry of the church.

Evangelism cells take the gospel into their neighbourhoods. These are people with a heart for their locality and a consequent desire to evangelise. The group meets to be trained in evangelism, to pray for the people they are targeting and then to arrange an opportunity for them to hear about Christ, maybe over dinner or after a tennis match. As people become Christians they can be cared for by that cell, as well as being added to the larger church body.

Social Action cells exist to express the care of Jesus. Groups are involved in helping the homeless, visiting elderly people, or working with children on a tough housing estate. These groups are like Jesus with his hands outstretched to a hurting world. Groups involved in this kind of ministry are not going to preach the gospel overtly but are showing the love of Jesus in a practical way. People will then share their testimony at an appropriate moment as the relationship develops.

Bible Study cells meet together to study God's word with the aim of being strengthened, grounded and released into the purposes of God. The groups discuss the Bible together so that every member is involved and enabled to grow. At a certain point group members may well feel that the time has come to be actively involved in a different type of cell and may leave the Bible study cell.

Training

Each of the leaders of these groups needs to be equipped. How do we teach people to lead someone to Christ? How do we organise events which non-Christians will feel a part of? How do we deal with the objections that people have to the Bible? And there are many more questions. A key factor in the development of these leaders is that many of them have undergone general training within our Bible school. However, they also get additional training in areas that relate specifically to small group ministry. The leaders receive such training on a regular basis and also have the opportunity to encourage each other through sharing in prayer and discussion.

Supervision

The power cells are divided up into geographical areas, each having a zonal leader. The power cell leaders receive support from these zonal leaders who pastor groups of seven or eight power cells. These zonal leaders are in turn pastored by one of the full time members of the pastoral team. Consequently leaders are continually receiving training but are also being cared for pastorally. When the leaders are equipped and strong, the groups function with great effect.

Each year many hundreds of people join Kensington Temple and it is vital that they become involved in the Power Cell programme. The rapid process of change and the large scale, action packed programme of the church means that the power cells are essential for the health and strength of the whole church. Power cells are not just an addition to an already busy programme, but are the cells of the body and a vital ingredient in the life and ministry of each individual and consequently of the city church itself. The groups are a microcosm of the whole. They evangelise, they care, they teach, and they show the love of Christ. But they do it in many hundreds of different locations and involve every member of the body. The people are truly becoming "doers of the word."

9

MONEY MATTERS

All over the world the harvest is ripening. In practically every continent God is moving in revival. Churches are being built, ministries are being raised up and projects are being developed for God's work. These are great days in which to be active for the Lord. God has placed into the hands of people in our generation great means by which the job can be done. We have global television networks, radio, video and mass literature production. Fast and efficient travel makes even the remotest parts of the world accessible. If ever there was a generation that could evangelise the world it is this one. We have the capacity to see the gospel preached to every person in the world by the end of the decade. There is a greater need today than ever before for resources to be poured into God's harvest.

Big churches and big Christian organisations are often being criticised for being big business. If you have a big vision, the likelihood is that you will also have a big budget. Christian stewardship will therefore mean careful handling of finance with all the disciplines of the best run business. But we take financial decisions based on the nature of the kingdom of God and not according to worldly business principles. We are not into profiteering or merchandising the word of God. We wish to generate finances in every biblically legitimate way, releasing gifted people into their ministry of giving, but above all we trust God to meet our needs.

God's resources

God has always made abundant provision for his work. He raises up exactly the right leadership and supplies the people power necessary to get the job done. He gives appropriate strategies for each situation, whether it is the apostle Paul blazing a trail for Christ across the ancient world or the urban missionary penetrating our modern housing estates. And, all along the way, he always makes sure his bills are paid. It is inconceivable that the Lord would ensure every other provision for his programme on earth and fail to enable his people to fulfil it financially. Surely he will equip us in every way to perform his will, and that includes material resources.

Wealth is an attribute of God; he is rich in every way. Even before he created the physical world God had all in himself. He holds all the treasures of wisdom, honour and power. The created world belongs to him. All its wealth and treasures are his. He made them to reflect his glory and surely can use them for his work in the world today. So often we think of these things as belonging to the devil, and this can breed a false spirituality that makes a virtue out of poverty.

> *"The earth is the Lord's and everything in it."*
>
> *(Psalm 24:1)*

It is true that Satan has made a rebellious bid to possess the wealth of the nations but we must never forget that God is the creator and Satan is a mere creature. When Satan's other temptation failed on Jesus, he tried to corrupt him through the offer of money and power

> *The devil led him up to a high place and showed him in an instant all the kingdoms of the world. [6]And he said to him, "I will give you all their authority and splendour, for it has been given to me, and I can give it to anyone I want to. [7]So if you worship me, it will all be yours." [8]Jesus answered, "It is written: 'Worship the Lord your God and serve him only.'"*
>
> *(Luke 4:5-8)*

Jesus' answer to the devil shows the bottom line as far as money is concerned. Nothing must ever take the place of God. Covetousness is idolatry and the love of money is the root of all evil.

> *"You cannot serve both God and Money."*
>
> *(Matthew 6:24)*

The words of Jesus are highly relevant for our modern secular materialistic societies, with their selfish economies and urban monuments to mammon. He said,

> *"What good will it be for a man if he gains the whole world, yet forfeits his soul? Or what can a man give in exchange for his soul? "*
>
> *(Matthew 16:26)*

These words should be written large across our greedy society today, as should also the warning Jesus gave when he told the parable of the rich fool.

> *"Watch out! Be on your guard against all kinds of greed; a man's life does not consist in the abundance of his possessions."*
>
> *(Luke 12:15)*

The rich fool had gained a high level of prosperity at the expense of his soul. He had everything as far as this world goes, but had nothing at all for the next life as his untimely death proved. Jesus' parable confronts all the madness of our 20th century materialism. Surely one thing is absolutely plain: we will never defeat the spirit of Mammon in our cities while we remain under its bondage. God will judge the complacent rich and greedy exploiters in the Church even more severely than those in the world.

However, these warnings concerning the dangers of wealth and the deceitfulness of riches have often been totally ignored by the Church. Some false teaching on prosperity suggests that your spirituality can be measured by how much money you have in the bank. This is obviously false and, so far, is not a significant problem in the British Church. We are more inclined towards the opposite (but equally dangerous) view which makes a spiritual virtue out of poverty. This poverty mentality is so entrenched in the British Church that it has become one of the most effective strongholds of Satan. As a result, God's work worldwide is being severely debilitated. We must destroy this attitude completely and clear it from our thinking.

Any thinking that prevents God's work from going forward is from the devil. It seems that some are more ready to believe the devil than they are to believe God. Do you remember Satan's words to Jesus? He said that all the authority and splendour of the kingdoms of the world belonged to him and that he held the power to give them to whoever he chose. But as the master of deceit, Satan was mixing truth with lies, and part truth with untruth. Jesus did not contradict Satan's arrogant statement, but that does not make his words true. Satan wanted Jesus to worship him, and he refused. What Satan claimed for himself is flatly contradicted elsewhere by Scripture. Much of the world's riches are owned and controlled by the godless, but this still does not discount the fact that God is in control and that honour and riches ultimately come from him.

God delights in bringing down the arrogant claims of the rich and powerful. The Babylonian emperor Nebuchadnezzar was blinded by his wealth and proudly believed he had achieved it all in his own strength. He said,

> *"Is not this the great Babylon I have built as the royal residence, by my mighty power and for the glory of my majesty?"*
>
> (Daniel 4:30)

The prophet Daniel had earlier warned the king what would happen. Nebuchadnezzar was going to be humbled by the removal of his sanity causing him to live like an animal until he recognised God's authority over his life. Daniel carefully explained why God was going to do this.

> *'The decision is announced by messengers; the holy ones declare the verdict, so that the living may know that the Most High is sovereign over the kingdoms of men and gives them to anyone he wishes and sets over them the lowliest of men.'*
>
> (Daniel 4:17)

King David also knew the true source of wealth and financial influence when he said to the Lord,

> *"Wealth and honour come from you; you are the ruler of all things. In your hands are strength and power to exalt and give strength to all."*
>
> (1 Chronicles 29:12)

Far from the popular impression that wealth is of the devil, and that poverty is a spiritual virtue, the Bible presents another picture. God is the God of wealth and we are to be grateful stewards of his resources. All this is of vital significance for us in the work of God today. The Lord is calling us to challenge not just our own faith for finances but also to confront the great financial institutions of our age and the spiritual forces that lie behind them. We are to bring down the stronghold of money and expose the foolishness of trusting in wealth and human wisdom. God is currently shaking the economies of the world, exposing the greed of the nations. World recession, massive budget deficits in the west, unbearable third world debts, unstable exchange rate mechanisms and banking systems are all evidence of the Divine shaking.

It is no co-incidence that all this is taking place against the background of worldwide Christian growth and expansion. He is shaking the confidence of the nations in the god of Mammon. And there is another, very exciting dimension. This shaking is beginning to cause the wealth of the nations to pour into the work of God making full provision for the building of his end-time temple.

Building the house of God

After the destruction of Jerusalem by the Babylonians and the seventy year exile, God raised up Cyrus, the pagan king of Persia, as his sovereign instrument to restore his people to the land of Judah. It is significant that God blessed Cyrus materially to get this job done.

> *"This is what the LORD says to his anointed, to Cyrus, whose right hand I take hold of to subdue nations before him and to strip kings of their armour, to open doors before him so that gates will not be shut: [2]I will go before you and will level the mountains; I will break down gates of bronze and cut through bars of iron. [3]I will give you the treasures of darkness, riches stored in secret places, so that you may know that I am the LORD, the God of Israel, who calls you by name. [4]For the sake of Jacob my servant, of Israel my chosen, I call you by name and bestow on you a title of honour, though you do not*

> *acknowledge me. [5]I am the LORD, and there is no other; apart from me there is no God. I will strengthen you, though you have not acknowledged me.*
>
> *(Isaiah 45:1-5)*

God raised up Cyrus even though he did not fully acknowledge God's power, and gave him political and financial influence over the world, throwing down the former Babylonian empire. In the process of this, God gave Cyrus the hidden treasures of darkness. Those riches that had been greedily stored away for many years were now brought out into the open and were utilised by the Lord for the outworking of his purposes through his people. Cyrus' triumph led directly to the restoration of the Jews to their land and the rebuilding of the temple, as is recorded in his royal decree,

> *This is what Cyrus king of Persia says: "The LORD, the God of heaven, has given me all the kingdoms of the earth and he has appointed me to build a temple for him at Jerusalem in Judah. [3]Anyone of his people among you - may his God be with him, and let him go up to Jerusalem in Judah and build the temple of the LORD, the God of Israel, the God who is in Jerusalem. [4]And the people of any place where survivors may now be living are to provide him with silver and gold, with goods and livestock, and with freewill offerings for the temple of God in Jerusalem."*
>
> *(Ezra 1:2-4)*

God will do the same thing in these last days. There is an enormous harvest to finance and a wonderful endtime temple to build. The Lord is going to make full provision for his Church today, just as he has always done. From the beginning God has always provided abundantly for the building of his house. He gave his people favour with the Egyptians who allowed themselves to be "plundered" by the Israelites. It was the back-pay for their years in slavery. His wealth enabled Moses to build the tabernacle in the wilderness. The provision was so plentiful that the people had to be restrained from bringing their offerings for the tabernacle (Exodus 36:6). The situation was repeated centuries later when king David made provision for the building of Solomon's temple. He gave vast resources from his royal treasury and his own personal funds for the work. The leaders and people of Israel followed his example and gave so willingly that there was abundant provision for the building of the temple.

Similar provision was made for the rebuilding of the house of God by Zerubbabel, though not at first. Those who remembered the glory of the former temple were disappointed when they saw the new house from the Lord. The prophet Haggai brought an encouraging promise of the Lord. The Lord affirmed his ownership over all things,

> *"The silver is mine and the gold is mine."*
>
> *(Haggai 2:8)*

He promised to shake the nations until their wealth poured into the temple. Then came the staggering word,

> *'The glory of this present house will be greater than the glory of the former house,' says the LORD Almighty. 'And in this place I will grant peace,' declares the LORD Almighty.*
>
> *(Haggai 2:9)*

We can expect nothing less than this today! God is going to perform such amazing financial miracles for the building of his endtime house. He will fully finance this harvest. We must believe him for the release of the wealth of the wicked stored up for the righteous. It is happening already. In the 1980's many western economies were flying high. Companies grew by greed and exploitation, financed largely by credit, and when many national economies fell into recession, property markets collapsed. Now in the 1990's churches are moving into the buildings vacated by bankrupt companies and are buying them for a fraction of the cost. As well as this, God is prospering Christian businesses in order to resource his work, and he is giving a new degree of acumen to skilled Christian financiers to raise vast sums of money for his work. This is a new day of God's provision. He is financing his Church so we can reap the worldwide endtime harvest.

The grace of giving

The endtime house of the Lord, however, will not just be financed by those with large scale businesses or special financial expertise. The Lord will empower ordinary Christians to be part of it. All God's great building programmes were financed through the freewill offering of his people. In the New Testament, giving is seen as a Christian grace or virtue which we are all called to excel in.

> *But just as you excel in everything—in faith, in speech, in knowledge, in complete earnestness and in your love for us—see that you also excel in this grace of giving.*
>
> *(2 Corinthians 8:7)*

This quality of giving lies at the heart of Christian character and is founded on the love God has shown in the giving of his Son to the world. It was demonstrated by Christ himself.

> *For you know the grace of our Lord Jesus Christ, that though he was rich, yet for your sakes he became poor, so that you through his poverty might become rich.*
>
> *(2 Corinthians 8:9)*

Such "grace-giving" must be seen in those who claim to walk with Jesus. In fact, how we give to God is often a clear indication of the state of our spiritual lives. It is not measured simply by the amount we give, but how that compares with what we are genuinely able to give and the motive in our hearts when we give. The widow in the gospel story gave more than all the wealthy givers when she put her offering in the temple treasury. Jesus pointed out,

> *They all gave out of their wealth; but she, out of her poverty, put in everything—all she had to live on.*
>
> *(Mark 12:44)*

The gift is acceptable to God on account of one's willingness to give and this is not necessarily seen in the size of the offering itself. The apostle Paul makes this clear when he instructs the church of Corinth concerning the offering. Giving must not be under duress, but must be the deliberate and joyful decision of the individual.

> *Each man should give what he has decided in his heart to give, not reluctantly or under compulsion, for God loves a cheerful giver.*
>
> *(2 Corinthians 9:7)*

Some have used this to teach against the practice of tithing, saying that we must only give as the Holy Spirit leads us. But Paul is not against the discipline of tithing. On the contrary, he established the correctness of giving in a planned and systematic way,

> *On the first day of every week, each one of you should set aside a sum of money in keeping with his income, saving it up, so that when I come no collections will have to be made.*
>
> *(1 Corinthians 16:2)*

Such an offering was in line with the practice of tithing taught in the Old Testament. Although it was part of the law of Moses, tithing is obviously not restricted to it. Abraham practised it centuries before the time of Moses, and the principle has applications for the building of the modern day house of the Lord. Tithing was given as means of provision for the Lord's house and we, the Church, are the Lord's house of the New Testament. Therefore tithing remains one of God's principle means of provision for the work of his Church today.

Biblical prosperity

We are often told that we should neither look for blessing nor expect rewards when giving. We must stand against the unbalanced teaching on of those who hold to the "prosperity gospel", but we must also be careful to make sure we have the balance right ourselves. After all, the Bible does teach prosperity. God does want to prosper his children. Obviously, as we have already seen, the Bible condemns covetousness; the love of money is spiritually disastrous. But God does bless his people financially in order to fulfil his purpose through them. You cannot out-give the Lord. He blesses those who honour him through generous giving.

> *One man gives freely, yet gains even more; another withholds unduly, but comes to poverty.* [25]*A generous man will prosper; he who refreshes others will himself be refreshed.*
>
> *(Proverbs 11:24,25)*

God wants you to discover the blessing of giving. He loves to reward faithfulness. As you give faithfully and generously to God's work, he promises to bless you and to prosper you. Biblical prosperity means having more than enough for your own needs so that you can minister to the needs of others. Giving to God must not be viewed as paying spiritual tax. Rather, it is an investment. And he gives good returns! As with any investment, the size of your return is determined by the size of the investment. Jesus outlined the principle,

> *"Give, and it will be given to you. A good measure, pressed down, shaken together and running over, will be poured into your lap. For with the measure you use, it will be measured to you."*
>
> *(Luke 6:38)*

Many people object to the idea of giving in order to get. Of course it is wrong to give with the ultimate aim of getting back for yourself, but it is absolutely right to expect God's rewards in giving. The motive must not be financial gain but financial empowering, making it possible for you to give all the more to God's work. After all, what farmer sows his seed without any thought for the harvest. If he wants an abundant harvest, he sows his seed liberally. In the same way we should sow our financial seed generously, looking for a harvest of blessing - both spiritual and financial, and therefore be equipped to be a greater blessing to God's people and God's work. Read the following passage carefully and see these principles at work. Notice the biblical balance between giving and receiving on the one hand and purity of motive on the other.

> *Remember this: Whoever sows sparingly will also reap
> sparingly, and whoever sows generously will also reap
> generously. [7]Each man should give what he has decided in his
> heart to give, not reluctantly or under compulsion, for God
> loves a cheerful giver. [8]And God is able to make all grace
> abound to you, so that in all things at all times, having all that
> you need, you will abound in every good work. [9]As it is written:
> "He has scattered abroad his gifts to the poor; his righteousness
> endures forever." [10]Now he who supplies seed to the sower and
> bread for food will also supply and increase your store of seed
> and will enlarge the harvest of your righteousness. [11]You will be
> made rich in every way so that you can be generous on every
> occasion, and through us your generosity will result in
> thanksgiving to God.*
>
> *(2 Corinthians 9:6-11)*

If we are going to see God's work in the cities across the nation adequately resourced, we must break free from a poverty mentality. It is time to let go of our unbiblical attitudes towards money and be bold in this area. We need a people of faith who know how to live according to God's promises for finance, giving according to the principles of his economy.

> *And my God will meet all your needs according to his glorious riches in Christ Jesus.*
>
> *(Philippians 4:19)*

10

CHRISTIAN UNITY

It has been my privilege to travel and minister in Africa, Asia, North and South America, Australia and the Far East. Everywhere I have gone I have literally marvelled at the wonder of this worldwide phenomenon called the Church. It must surely be one of the greatest demonstrations of the truth of Christianity. In many places, such as China and the former Soviet Union, the Church has recently passed through some of the greatest persecutions known to man this century, but has emerged stronger than ever. Every day in China more than 25,000 find Christ and thousands of people are accepting the Christian message in Russia. Even former KGB agents who until recently times were duty bound to confiscate Bibles are now themselves hungry for Christian literature!

But it is not just the strength of the Church today that is impressive. I never cease to be amazed at the unity in the Spirit which is our birthright as Christians. We can meet each other anywhere in the world and instantly there is that bond of recognition; we are brothers and sisters in the Lord. Instantly recognisable in any language, the words "Hallelujah" and "Amen" echo in praise of Christ all over the world. This unity is all the more remarkable when you look at the diversity of the Church. We are one body, but many members. And each member, unique in itself, is a genuine part of the mystery which is his body. In the Church, Christ shines uniquely through every particular culture and every individual person, whatever his race or nationality. We have so much to learn from each other. Every expression of the Church, whether in Britain or across the nations, is both valid and valuable.

The same is true of the church within a city. Most modern cities are cosmopolitan and carry many different cultures and many more subcultural groups. There are many expressions of the body of Christ within most cities which all uniquely reflect the face of Jesus. Denominational streams flowing in the city can refresh us all and we need to grow in our appreciation of this fact. It seems to me that diversity is what makes our unity so valuable. How boring it would be if we were all the same. No one church or denomination holds all that Christ is but each is a part of the greater whole. This means we cannot even think of going it alone as it would be a fundamental denial of the nature of the Church and therefore, ultimately of the gospel itself.

If all this is true, how can we work better together? What will true unity look like? How will we stand with others so that the world may believe Jesus Christ is alive? Christian unity can be compared to the unity that exists between the persons of the Godhead - God the Father, Son and Holy Spirit. These three persons are one God, and therefore we cannot press the analogy too far, but the unity of the Trinity forms the pattern for our unity as believers. In John 17, Jesus prays for the unity of the Church, and twice he says that they may be one even as we are one (John 17:11,22). What kind of unity then, exists between the Father and the Son and indeed all the members of the

Trinity? I recognise three aspects to this Divine unity that shows us the nature of the unity of the Church.

Unity in nature

The Father and Son are one. That is, one in nature, substance and essence, and their relationship is based on this fundamental unity. The Father and Son are not one because they come together in relationship, but they are in relationship because they share a deeper underlying oneness; they are of the same substance. Father, Son and Holy Spirit are all fully God and share equally in the Divine nature. In the same way, Christian unity comes from sharing in the nature of Christ. Our communion comes from our union in Christ. We are in relationship with each other because we are in relationship with him. Our coming together does not make us one, but we come together as an expression of the unity we already have in Christ. Our unity is a unity in the truth, that is, the truth about Jesus and the truth that is Jesus. Again this is a reflection of the Divine unity as Jesus says to the Father,

> *"I in them and you in me."*
>
> *(John 17:23)*

Christian unity has only one basis - relationship with Jesus Christ. It is gospel unity and rests on the foundation of the gospel alone.

Unity in purpose

The Father and the Son are totally united in plan and purpose. They are always going in the same way and never pull in different directions. There is complete co-operation between the members of the Trinity, but this does not exclude diversity of function. While the persons of the Godhead work together on everything, they do not all have precisely the same function. There is a distribution of responsibility and a diversity of function in the Trinity. The Father is the Divine initiator, the great master planner of the Trinity. The Son fulfils the will of the Father, always in submission, though he is equal to the Father. And the Holy Spirit is the great executive of the Godhead. He executes the word of the Father and the Son, while of course always remaining fully Divine himself.

This means that our unity as Christians will give rise to co-operation rather than competition. It would be unthinkable for the members of the Trinity to be competing with each other. Rather, they co-operate fully and equally share the Divine glory. The Father glorifies the Son and the Son glorifies the Father and the Holy Spirit glorifies both the Father and the Son. This should be reflected in all our churches, denominations and streams today. There should be no criticism of each other (wherever do we read of the Son criticising the Father), there should be no jealousy or maligning of each other. Instead, we should truly honour one another and prefer one another in love. All this comes from a healthy recognition of other churches with their God-given roles. As we seek to understand the place God has given to each of us we will be enriched by the diversity. Instead of trying to make everyone conform to our styles and methods, we will be free to fulfil our part in the total plan of God. It also means that there must be no independence, but a clearly-acknowledged interdependence, each church being an active part of the overall strategy.

Unity in mission

This is the true goal of unity. The mission of God is to reach out and rescue the world from sin. Therefore unity that does not truly lead to mission is not unity at all. Counterfeit unity is content with getting together in small-minded and suspicious meetings, with ministers expressing superficial courtesies in fraternals and with the observance of inter-church pulpit etiquette. Meantime the world lunges headlong into hell. The true purpose of God's unity is for mission. Jesus made this abundantly clear,

> *May they be brought to complete unity to let the world know that you sent me and have loved them even as you have loved me.*
>
> (*John* 17:23)

Some speak in glowing terms of their near magical vision of unity. Driven by an ethereal dream that lies at the very edges of deception, they speak of the results they expect. Frankly, the world is not in the least bit impressed by Christian get-togethers. Jesus was speaking of what we should do when we get together. We are to join together to win the world through evangelism and mission. It is a call for united practical action. In some circles today unity is seen almost as a end in itself and is being relentlessly pursued without the least thought to its real purpose. The results are disastrous. The gospel purpose for unity is so far removed from some churches' thinking that they are speaking of an ecumenical unity that has no place for gospel truth. We are being called upon to unite with groups which deny Christ and his message, and to attend gatherings where Christian truth is watered down to nothing. We need biblical unity which is vibrant and full-blooded, not meeting around the lowest common denominational denominators. In some places, Christians are even expected to take their place alongside others whose beliefs deny the lordship and saviourhood of Jesus Christ. We are in danger of the sin of Esau, and if we are not careful we will sell our birthright as biblical Christians for a bowl of ecumenical soup.

But the danger is not just in the ecumenical movement. Some evangelical moves for unity also put us at risk. One evangelical group of churches I know recently began to define narrow geographical boundaries, which effectively killed off evangelistic and church planting initiatives within what they called "their" area! Christian unity must be outward looking, not inward and defensive. Genuine unity will lead to evangelistic outreach initiatives and the proliferation of vibrant and growing churches.

Working together

How can Christians work together to win their cities for Jesus Christ? How do citywide initiatives affect what is already happening through local churches? We at Kensington Temple have our own comprehensive plan for reaching London with the gospel but we are not the only ones with a London-wide strategy. That is why we work in co-operation with others; we could never do it alone. Nobody can speak of competition when 90% of people are not being touched by any church. There is plenty of scope out there and more than enough sinners to go round. It is vital to create a network of our resources so that we can all work together to win the city. To do this with complete confidence and without the fear of losing our own identity and vision, we must be secure in our own call.

At present, Kensington Temple is in co-operation with six other groups which have a strong commitment to reach London. This is not a new superchurch or any institution in embryo, but simply a network of leaders whose churches and church groups all have a heart for London. In addition to the links Kensington Temple has through its own denomination with other Elim Pentecostal churches in London, we are also standing with leaders such as Gerald Coates of Pioneer, Roger Forster of Ichthus, Lynn Green of Youth With A Mission and Sandy Millar of Holy Trinity Brompton. Strong relationships are being developed with other churches as well. Personally, I value my contact and fellowship with many other London leaders. In addition to this we are receiving frequent input and encouragement from national and international ministries to whom God has given a prophetic message for London. In all of this, we keep our integrity as a specific move of God, or stream in the city. We know that we cannot win London on our own. The whole church must reach the whole city. However, with the help of gifts and ministries from the wider body we will play our part.

Local churches and citywide strategies

Many people question the idea of citywide strategies. It can sound like an attempt to impose something from the top or from outside onto local leaders. For instance, many London leaders have a local vision and do not think in terms of London-wide strategies. How do the two approaches correlate? First of all, the key is in the hands of local pastors. As we work side by side, in our given locality, a co-operative strategy emerges which in turn discernibly develops into a wider pattern. This can then penetrate the city as a whole. At the same time, the citywide strategies must be broken down into local initiatives. Both approaches can serve each other. Local efforts are likely to be much nearer the grass roots and more effective at a community level while, on the other hand, citywide strategies are usually able to keep the overall objective in view, providing much-needed encouragement and resources to local groups.

Territorial restrictions

One way frustration often develops in inter-church co-operation is through the imposition of parochial limitations. Most local churches have inherited outmoded concepts of church boundaries. Often these have long since ceased to hold any practical or sociological significance. City-dwellers are mobile and are no longer territorial in their life-style. They live, work, shop, are entertained, and even worship in almost as many different areas as there are categories of activity. And yet many churches are still bound by a territorial mentality. A territorial approach ignores the importance of social networks in reaching the people of the city and at worst views co-operation between churches as defining and defending "my patch." Church leaders will never see the true power of Christian unity between local churches if they are simply intent on defending their patch.

Local churches must accept responsibility for their local areas. However, when they foster a spiritual closed-shop mentality and reject others whom the Lord may also be calling into the area, they are just as wrong as the outside group which crashes ahead with its vision, irrespective of the local churches which are already in existence.

Honouring vision

A far better basis for co-operation is to seek to honour the vision that the Lord has given to each church group. Any apparent conflict of interest should be resolved in a spirit of facilitation and not defensiveness. Often we don't even see the relevance of someone else's vision because we are too caught up in our own, falsely believing that there is nothing beyond what we have seen. When it comes to church planting, I have found there is a people-blindness which often exists in leaders. Local churches think that they are reaching the community and resent others coming into the area, but I know of no community in London which has enough churches to cater for the number of people and cultures that exist even within half a square mile. We need many different types of church in every area, reflecting all its cultural and social groups.

We must learn to recognise the heartbeat of God in each other and acknowledge that what God is doing through others is equally important as what he is doing through us. Above all there must be real openness and flexibility in all our thinking. This is the only way we are truly going to hear the Lord and be ready to reach more than 50 million people in our nation who are without Christ.

11

TIME FOR ACTION

As this book reaches its final pages it is your opportunity for a new beginning. It is possible to read this book and welcome its vision and direction. It is also possible to read this book and be drawn to your knees in prayer. Both of these responses are good; however, neither of these responses is enough. It is time for the people of God to take their place of authority in the city. It is time for the city to change and it is time for the Church to change it.

In this book I have shown something of God's heart for the city of London. The vision and dreams that God has imparted make clear that his will is to win the city rather than just to build a large church. God wants to build a church that affects the city's politics, the way that children are taught in school, the way the poor are cared for, the way finance is shared around and so much more. I am sure that every Christian who reads this book would desire to live in that kind of city. But the question is, "Are you willing to pay the price for it to happen?" Are you prepared to give the time, energy, resources and commitment to see the will of God accomplished? The cost will be great but the results will change your life and the lives of your children and your children's children.

The opportunities are vast; the responsibilities are great. Imagine with me Christians called by God to serve him in parliament, in the classroom, in the board room, as doctors and nurses, in factories and in the police force; thousands of Christians responding to God's call to penetrate every stratum of society; pockets of light all over the city getting brighter and brighter and brighter; light overcoming darkness in our schools; light overcoming darkness in parliament; light overcoming darkness in the city of London; light overcoming darkness in your city; and then those individual lights coming together to stand as the city church; a church of the nations ministering to the city; a church of faith, celebration, healings, spiritual gifts, prayer, social help; a church where the glory of God is present!

Can it happen? The good news is that it is already happening all over the world and it is beginning to happen here in Britain. Thousands and thousands of others are going to have a part in fulfilling God's plan for the cities. First we need to recognise that God's call is so much bigger than we have realised. God has a unique call for each one of us, not just for those who are going to become pastors or teachers.

Find out God's specific plan for you - what your strategic role is in this great advance of the kingdom. Whatever job God has called you to do, be it a local councillor, labourer, nurse, factory worker or teacher, then fulfil your ministry under the anointing of the Holy Spirit. Take the kingdom of God into your workplace and let God empower you to see the city church built there.

Will we see the full extent of the city church vision described in this book? God certainly wants it and he is willing to transfer every bit of power and authority that we need to get the job done. The question is not about God but about us. So often the task has been left to a spiritual elite but this never was and never will be God's plan. God wants each of us to discover our place in the body and then to function effectively. I challenge you to seek God and to ask him, "What must I do to respond to your heart for the city?" He wants your availability. It is time for action!

Notes